W9-BGN-084

Advance Praise for *Live Ablaze*

"Gut-wrenching in candor and replete with vision, this book is both lifeline and roadmap for those who want more … for themselves, for those they love, and for those they've never met. If you are ready to look wide-eyed into your own soul and begin to live life ablaze, read this book!"

-Deborah Rohan, Author of *One Person Acted and Everything Changed: 10 Inspiring Accounts of World Changers*, Founder & CEO of One Person Acted (onepersonacted.com)

"A masterpiece in every way. *Live Ablaze and Light Up the World* is not 'just another book,' it is a 'must read' work of art that you simply won't want to put down. It draws you in like a magnet, stirs your emotions and remains close to your heart. As you turn the pages, and work through the PoPs, you will find yourself smiling, crying, laughing, searching, pausing, reflecting, listening and discovering … lighting your fire and unleashing your greatness!"

-Melissa Schaap, VP of Connections & Partnerships of IMANI COLLECTIVE (imanicollective.com)

"*Live Ablaze* is a refreshing nudge to BE. To BE, without taking yourself too seriously, but seriously enough to share your passion and gifts. To transform past hurts into beautiful gifts, and to share those gifts in a giant leap forward with a tribe of trusted 'soul friends'!"

-Michelle Sugerman, Founder & CEO of Leading Synergies (leadingsynergies.com)

"In this oh-so-relevant and beautifully written book, Sarah encourages us to reclaim what is our own unique *jOURney*. The experience for me was an inner unfolding of sorts that left me with a deep sense of both relief and belonging. In the sacred space that Sarah so carefully creates for us, we find the nuggets of truth and wisdom that hold the pathway for us to understand why we are here and what we need to do.

The pages have us not only discovering what can be uncovered (or rediscovered) in ourselves, but Sarah reminds us that we belong to each other as well—and by connecting with this bigger human family, our hopes and dreams can be accelerated even further. Reading this book falls into the category of genuinely giving to yourself."

-Lydia Dean, co-founder of GoPhilanthropic Foundation (gophilanthropic.org) and author of *Jumping the Picket Fence: A Woman's Search for Meaning from the Suburbs to the Slums*

"If you have met Sarah, you know the magic, sparkle and love that she exudes. Being in the same room always brings more love and grace into my life ... since I can't move into Sarah's home permanently, *Live Ablaze* is the next best thing to expanding my life with her light!"

-Angela Melfi, co-founder of Threads Worldwide (threadsworldwide.com)

Live ablāze

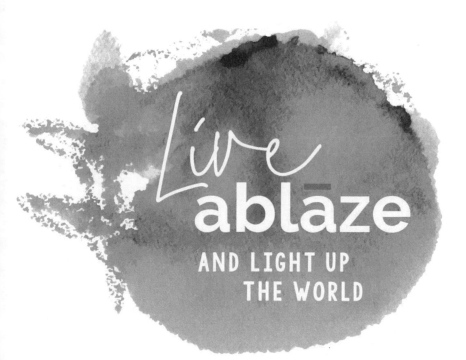

Live
ablāze

AND LIGHT UP THE WORLD

SARAH DAVISON-TRACY

IGNITE!
PUBLISHERS

Live Ablaze: And Light Up the World
Published by Ignite Publishers
Denver, CO

Copyright ©2018 SARAH DAVISON-TRACY. All rights reserved.

No part of this book may be reproduced in any form or by any mechanical means, including information storage and retrieval systems without permission in writing from the publisher/author, except by a reviewer who may quote passages in a review.

All images, logos, quotes, and trademarks included in this book are subject to use according to trademark and copyright laws of the United States of America.

Library of Congress Control Number: 2018903927
DAVISON-TRACY, SARAH, Author
Live Ablaze
Sarah Davison-Tracy

ISBN: 978-0-9997212-0-9

BODY, MIND & SPIRIT / Inspiration & Personal Growth
SELF-HELP / Personal Growth / General
PHILOSOPHY / Movements / Idealism

COVER DESIGN: ASTRID KOCH

AUTHOR PHOTO: J RENAE DAVIDSON

INTERIOR LAYOUT: ANDREA COSTANTINE

QUANTITY PURCHASES: Schools, companies, professional groups, clubs, and other organizations may qualify for special terms when ordering quantities of this title. For information, email Info@IgnitePublishers.com.

All rights reserved by Sarah Davison-Tracy and Ignite Publishers. This book is printed in the United States of America.

To the One whose Love planted the seeds of this story in my heart.
This work is all Yours—I am all Yours.

Brandon, your jaw-dropping cheerleading
and limitless love stuns and humbles me.

Soph and Micah, you two make my heart thrum with
pride, inspiration, and joy.

xo
Sarah DT

Contents

BE BOLD. BE BRAVE. BE YOU.

[we begin]

welcome

Welcome,
dear friend.
I've been expecting you.

Do you know there is
more than a bit of destiny
in this moment?

To be sure, this is no accident.
Mighty wheels have been set in motion,
propelling you on the adventure of a lifetime.

Our time together in these pages
will kindle your highest hopes
and most audacious dreams.
So ... jOURney on.

Crafted with you in Mind

YES, IT'S TRUE. THIS BOOK HAS BEEN CRAFTED, FROM START TO FINISH, WITH YOU IN MIND.

I envision these pages to feel like a cozy conversation between friends over steaming cups of chai tea or refreshing icy drinks ... or as if we are taking a beach walk together, our toes digging into the cool sand and the waves gently covering our feet with froth as we meander along the shoreline.

I imagine us journeying together, as you come along with me to meet some extraordinary people, some of whom can be found in my neighborhood, while others live in far-off parts of the world. As we go, you will be astonished at the ease with which their stories connect with and illuminate your own.

I invite you to say *YES!* to this quest, an experience of claiming your one-of-a-kind purpose on the planet, wholeheartedly connecting with your expansive human family members near and far, and cultivating a vision for your part in lighting up the world. This adventure of a lifetime is planted in each and every person, making for companions aplenty along the road.

One step at a time, you will uncover more of who you are, what you want to do, why and with whom you do it. Even when the path is hard and confusing, when your purpose seems more foggy than crystal clear, this very purpose pulsates within you. It pulsates with power to fuel your steps in breathtaking ways. It pulsates and beckons you to keep walking, to trust that you are here with a one-of-a-kind gift—one that our world greatly needs—and to become more deeply connected than ever to others as you go.

The promise of such a journey is that you will experience more moments that take your breath away. Your life will captivate your attention in ways you never before imagined. You will be on the edge of your seat with excitement, standing on your tiptoes with anticipation, as the glow of hope, peace, and joy radiate within, stoking the flames of a life far beyond what you ever dared to dream.

Our Travel Itinerary

THIS JOURNEY THAT YOU ARE ABOUT TO BEGIN HAS BEEN BROKEN DOWN INTO FOUR TRAVEL SEGMENTS.

Each segment described below represents an essential part of the complete journey.

(1) KINDLING. The first leg of our adventure is all about excitement and the ripples of possibility.

(2) FLICKERING. In this part of our journey, the pace will slow way down, as we gently tend to places of real-life struggles. Rooted in hope, we will search for and find ways that this very heartbreak offers a treasure trove of astounding gifts.

(3) SPARKING. This leg of our journey swells with emotion and energy as we discover various expressions of a life well-lived.

Here, you may catch a glimpse of the ways your life can become more sparking and sparkling than ever.

(4) BLAZING. As you reach the final segment of our adventure, booming and beautiful fireworks will light up your path. Get ready to celebrate a vision for your part in the world that sets your life ablaze beyond your wildest dreams.

As we travel together in and through each of these parts, know that this journey is yours to direct. If you find yourself inclined to stay in one place a bit longer, stay. If you're ready to move along, do it. There is no right or wrong pace—travel forward in your unique way. We each move at different tempos ... honor and cultivate your own.

your Tour Guide

I DO NOT HAVE THE MAP FOR YOU, BUT I DO HAVE A FEW PLACES I WANT YOU TO VISIT AND PEOPLE I WANT YOU TO MEET.

I do not have answers for the questions that may arise, but I do have some curiosities and ideas about what to do with the quandaries.

Along the way, I share tools and wisdom that have kept me going in the midst of the always twisting and turning path of life.

As we begin, here is a glimpse of who I am and why this invitation to travel together matters to me.

I love celebrating cultures and my global human family. As a mother, I love these young ones—these children of mine. Caring for them has burst open my heart, beckoned me to let go, to be emptied of—and yet find—myself in such a way that I now fly, rise, and soar less encumbered.

As a pilgrim, I love deepening my relationship with and experiences of the Sacred in more bits of life each day, saying yes to my purpose on the planet more often and more deeply, being held by the One who loves me most, in Whose ocean of grace I float free and am at peace.

As a world traveler, I love airports, passport in my pocket, new currency in my wallet, tastes on my tongue, languages in my ears, and fabrics on my skin, new-to-me sisters and brothers who capture and expand my heart.

> You will be on the edge of your seat with excitement, standing on your tiptoes with anticipation, as the glow of hope, peace, and joy radiate within, stoking the flames of a life far beyond what you ever dared to dream.

These people and passions inspired and propelled me to create Seeds of Exchange (seedsofexchange.org), a collective of everyday people who are committed to light up the world so that a mighty difference can be made together. We do what we do because we believe that we belong to each other and that each and every person matters. We passionately work to make an indelible dent in global human rights and in one another's day-to-day lives.

Travel Tenets

BELOW ARE A FEW WAYS TO THINK ABOUT AND ENGAGE WITH THIS ADVENTURE.

They are core tenets you will encounter to enrich and provide structure for the days ahead. Whether these are familiar and already in your toolkit for navigating life or brand new to you, I hope they encourage, illuminate, and fuel your next steps and future leaps.

Stories change us ... and our world. They quiet and teach us to sit, to listen, to speak, to be heard, and to be seen. They invite us to comprehend and claim our own story anew as we take in the stories of others. They open doors within us to see possibilities for building community and connection, for creating simple and robust daily rhythms, and for cultivating meaningful work. The most powerful stories occur in the *everydayness* and nitty-gritty of life. Ultimately, stories change us and the world as they evoke more of *who we are* in thought, word, and action.

The local and global are each important. We will explore ways to simply serve and be present to those both near and far. Each person's unique purpose on the planet may have an essence of one, both, or a mysterious mixture of this local-global flavor. Here's the thing: one is not better than the other. Our world needs people who are deeply dedicated to both our neighborhoods and distant lands.

The words we use matter. In these pages, grammar rules have been broken. I frolic a bit with capitalization and italics, sometimes capitalizing words within words I want to emphasize. It is meant to convey a sense of energy in the words—to reach out from the pages and greet you; to say, for example, "Hello there, are you ready to be *COURAGEous*?"

There are also many *both-ands* in these pages, including giving and receiving, contemplating (*BEing*) and acting (*DOing*), solitude and community, and waiting and leaping. These *both-ands* invite surprising epiphanies and the opportunity to experience yourself more fluid, free, and flexible than ever.

The word *good* is used throughout the *jOURney* ahead. Here, it is not a vanilla, washed out, or bland sentiment. Far from it. This *goodness* is the feeling of *ahh* when you kick back in one of your favorite places, with a sigh of satisfaction and bliss escaping softly smiling lips.

Woo-woo works (often). According to the Merriam-Webster dictionary, woo-woo is "dubiously or outlandishly mystical, supernatural, or unscientific." I get it. There is a lot of woo-woo that seems wacky and disconnected from much of life. But, when grounded into the soil of your everyday life, woo-woo can, and often does, work. There are many bits of life that beckon and benefit from opening to approaches other than those logical, linear, and familiar. So, my friend, if you are struck by something that seems a bit woo-woo, try it on and see how it fits.

Live *emBOLDened* in the midst of the unknown. It is a deeply natural and exceedingly common human tendency to believe that for life to be *good* and meaningful, for you to live free and at ease, to be clear about what matters most to you in life, all kinds of external measurables of clarity and success must happen first. *But ... it need not be.* Consider that a life ablaze does not depend on *KNOWing* and seeing clearly. Within the uncertainty, you can live with your head held high and with unabashed confidence right here and now.

There are powerful metaphors evidenced in the natural world. They can speak to us in the ebb and flow of the ocean tides, in the changing of the seasons, in the cycle of life and death, and in the magnificent multiplying effect of plants. Seeds are a real-life example of just how generative life can be. These growing things remind me that there is often a great deal happening even when things look dead or haven't yet begun to appear on the surface. Life is often being strengthened under the soil where we can't yet see it.

Navigating life alone doesn't work. It is essential to have a tribe of trusted companions with whom there is a commitment to *keep it real* and to wholly love. If you do not yet have a trusted community of a few or many, never fear, because that's part of this road. By the end of this quest, you will have considered and decided which steps to take to build your own tribe of people with whom you navigate the always changing seasons: the hard and easy, the *beautyFULL* and the painful.

The Real Gold: pops

I HAVE CRAFTED AN EXPERIENCE OF TEN POPS (PLACES OF PAUSE) WITHIN THIS JOURNEY TOGETHER.

They are a radically simple—simply radical—way to fuel your life, stilling the noise and promoting plentiful peace. They are sojourns on the road— beautiful and restorative resting places to cultivate energy to emerge up and out of the soil.

Each of the ten PoPs has three parts: *Be Still*, *Ponder*, and *Engage*. They are opportunities for contemplation and action. The times to *Be Still* and *Ponder* are all about intention and attention. Refreshment is found here. They offer moments to cultivate discernment, thoughtful planning, and momentum for change. Your inspiration to *Engage* will be rooted in the stability and wisdom you cultivate in stillness and pondering, free of the frantic or forceful energy that often accompanies quests for transformation. You may find yourself excited to act in big or small, local or global ways. Whatever the scale, the locale, and the perceived impact, what comes to you will be *life-changing*, *peace-making*, *bridge-building*, and *change-making*.

These PoPs are profound. They will meet you just where you are. Whether you're worn out from operating for too long in service and action without a moment to catch your breath, or you've been too long stuck and stationary, you will discover just what you need in your PoPs. This is about a solitude that kindles, not an extended isolation that saps.

The possibilities for you within these PoPs are infinite. Freely tweak your engagement with these prompts in a way that most compels you. There is no right or wrong way to do this. There is no need to force anything here. What to do will take shape, solidify, come into focus, and light up your next steps at just the right time. As you spend time being still, pondering, and engaging, your life will become even more stunning, *beautyFULL*, and uniquely yours.

Your ever-unfolding story and next steps will be revealed *by you* within these ten PoPs. Breakthrough and epiphany reside here. Watch for them. Count on them. This is where the fire of your life is stoked.

Integrating PoPs into a daily practice, or even a few times throughout the day, makes you more able to respond less reactively, less fearfully, with deep wisdom. For a glimpse at how these rhythms of PoPs look in my everyday life, I start my mornings with a PoP that always involves a steaming cup of coffee, a lit candle, my journal and sacred text, the Bible, while the house is quiet and before I jump into the day's demands.

> The world gives itself up to incessant activity merely because it knows of nothing better. The inspired man works among its whirring wheels also, but he knows whither the wheels are going. For he has found the centre where all is stillness...
> -Paul Brunton

Sometimes it's ten minutes; sometimes it's an hour. At midday, I pause for another PoP, and I head outside for a few minutes to take in some fresh air or read something that inspires me. (This one takes the most discipline for me to honor, and yet, it never fails to refresh me.) At night, before I go to sleep, I take a final PoP to review my day and prepare for the day ahead, paying attention to any niggling bits of worry or unresolved challenges, and surrender them to the Sacred. I always end with one or two things to be grateful for. These PoPs are done within the context of a full-to-the-brim life of family, work, vacation, sickness, the unplanned and unexpected, the minutia of to dos. They bookend and fuel my days.

What would it be like for you to create your own practice of PoP? Perhaps using this framework as a starting point, but tweaking it a bit to make it your own? Consider including these three elements: *Be Still*, *Ponder*, and *Engage*. Time to be still—not thinking, strategizing, or planning, but just *BEing*. Time to ponder—to reflect, to contemplate—going a level or two deeper into your life, panning for the gold and the glimmer within you. Time to engage—to work these moments of stillness and pondering into your life—to explore, to experiment, and to see what's working and what's not, in connection with your tribe and companioned by your own relationship with the Sacred. Whatever you do, never go it alone.

> Integrating PoPs into a daily practice, or even a few times throughout the day, makes you more able to respond less reactively, less fearfully, with deep wisdom.

What might this look like for you? Is it a certain time of day …. or times of day? What would it be like to take the triggers that come your way during the day—worry, fear, opportunity, decisions to make, relationships to negotiate, people you love who are in pain and in need of support—and take these into a PoP? To take some quiet time to get still, contemplate, and listen for nudges rooted in wisdom and the realities of your life here and now? I believe this will be a game-changer for you, a practice that will deeply kindle and sustain your radiant *life ablaze*.

I invite you to play with this framework and make it your own as you navigate life, whether feeling brave or afraid, lamenting or joyful. It is a practice that cultivates a way of life in which you can tend to what you most need, which is always changing: your next steps, refreshment, encouragement, action, community, and more.

Buckle Up

SO, ARE YOU READY TO PRESS ON ... WALKING, FLYING, AND LIFTING OFF TOGETHER?

Whether you feel more-than-ready, with a sense that you have been waiting for such an invitation for a long time, or you barely have energy for such a life, you are in just the right spot.

You may feel burdened by giant personal or global happenings. You may lack energy for anything beyond your daily needs and obligations. You may wonder whether you have enough to share that will make a difference. If so, not to worry. You are not alone—many of us are right here with you. Journey on. You belong here.

The way may not always be clear, and obstacles will likely emerge along the way, but regardless, we're going to walk, one step at a time, together, through the challenges that abound. It is because of and within these exceedingly real, everyday human struggles that I invite you on this *jOURney*.

Even if you weren't really planning on this sort of an adventure, consider it a free, surprise trip. No matter if you're already adept at adventuring or not, there are wonders aplenty in the discoveries to be made for even the most seasoned travelers. You have been preparing for this moment of liftoff. You wouldn't be here if it were not so. It's time.

1

[kindling]

exciting. stirring up. starting a
fire animating. rousing. inflaming
lighting up. illuminating. making
bright.

what's possible for you?

You are what the world has been waiting for
in all your real-ness and splendor-ness.
Sometimes all it takes is a bit of fuel to get
that fire going.

In the economy of love's ways,
there is always plenty.
With love as the fuel for who you are
and for what you do,
you are more than enough.

Your dreams and desires are
where your vision, your what,
and your why are planted,
where you come alive and where
the crescendo of your life is fueled.
Your purpose on the planet is rooted here.

The time is now to kindle your dreams
—whether brand new or old—
and strengthen your heart
to believe that the time is now.
As you do, get ready for the sonic boom
that will set your life aglow.

Limitless Love

LOVE. IT IS A TRAVEL ESSENTIAL ON THIS ROAD TO ALL THAT IS POSSIBLE.

The lens of limitless love allows you to see your next steps and leaps that will lead toward your big dreams and unique inspired purpose on the planet—in your backyard and in distant lands.

Limitless love invites you to live *BEloved*.

Living *BEloved* fuels you to be love. Always. Not always immediately, but always. It knows when you've been strengthened enough and have filled up enough to be ready for the delight to be love to those around you. It is not a burdensome doing; it is like a dance, like a song, and it is joyful. When this plentiful love is the primary fuel for who you are and what you do, your passion, strength, and courage will be more than enough. Always enough. In the economy of love's ways, there is perpetually plenty.

Living *BEloved* is wise and knows that too much self-love or too much other-love sucks the *joie de vivre* (French, for "the pure joy of living") from you. This love is fierce, smashing to smithereens the message that you need to *do* more to be loved, to belong, and to have value, freeing you to just *be* you and to be energized to do things for others.

Living *BEloved* frees you to be loved and to love like never before. This love has deep roots that are strong and far-reaching and will nudge you toward whatever it is you need each moment of each day, creating a rhythm of deep internal sustainability. Its tendrils grow within you so wholly that you are profoundly changed. They grow up and out of you, brushing up against those closest to and furthest from you.

This is not a weak-sauce, syrupy, nice, or sweet love. It is not hippy-dippy or esoteric. Sappy love barely cuts it on the easy days, and it certainly doesn't sustain when the going gets tough. Sappy love is also boring. Boring is secure and safe, but it will not have you leaning forward, riveted with attention and eagerness, owning your life with authority and confidence, with your head thrown back, your hair blowing in the wind, and your voice strong and mighty, declaring and living what matters to you.

> Perhaps here people are materially well off, but I think if we looked inside the houses we should find that it is difficult sometimes to smile at each other, even though such a smile might be the beginning of love. For this reason, we always greet each other with a smile, because it is the beginning of love, and when one begins to love it is natural to want to do something.
> -Mother Teresa, *Mother Teresa: Her Life Her Works*

This limitless love is pervasive. It resides everywhere, within the moments of richer and poorer, sickness and health, sameness and difference, overwhelm and peace, isolation and togetherness, division and unification. Whether you feel you have been kicked in the gut or are lit up with joy, love is there—love is *here*. This love is the oxygen you need to breathe when you feel you are suffocating and the whisper you need to hear when you don't know how much longer you can make it.

I invite you to be launched by this limitless love in more bits of life. When love moves you to wade into painful, hopeless, and forgotten places, the ripples that emerge from this courageous way of life are difference-making, not only in the world, but in you.

Dreams & Desires

WHEN YOU DREAM BIG, YOU ARE AWAKE. YOU ARE STRONG AND FIERCE.

You hold your head high; your eyes are direct and focused. You speak clearly about what matters to you.

You keep it real, and you look for and find the same in others. You are at peace among the oft' present imperfections, discomfort, and unknown. Fog and confusion lessen … and they don't matter so much when they do come into view. You listen and act with conviction and inspiration. You discover that the things that have separated you from yourself and others decrease. The ways you think and talk about what matters in life is captivating and expansive.

Tending to and fanning the flames of your dreams and desires are some of the starting points for our *jOURney*. Look for them. Explore them. Trust them, my friend. Yes, trust them, whether itty-bitty or whopping dreams. They offer some clues for your unfolding story.

And, my friend, share them, too. Yes, your dreams are meant to be shared. They rarely grow when kept inside you. They need to be brought out into the open, to be spoken, to be exposed to the light of day and the real in the world. Sharing your dreams can be daunting and leave you feeling vulnerable, and yet, what happens as a result of sharing them is pure magic. *You will be lit up.*

It may feel as though your dreams are dormant. You may have become disconnected from your sense of your palpable purpose.

Or maybe you don't see a way to connect those dreams with your everyday life. Not to worry. They are with you right now. They may just need a bit of nurturing, of gentle encouragement to c'mon out. In Nepal, they have a word I love, particularly when it comes to things like this that cannot be rushed or forced. It is *bistari*, which means "slowly." *Bistari* gives us permission to move gently, intentionally, and without rushing.

> Let yourself be
> drawn by
> the pull of what
> you really love.
> -Rumi

My friend, whether you have a hunch, no idea at all, or laser clarity about your small or big dreams, I'm cheering you on. Wherever you find yourself right here and now is good—it is plenty. More will be discovered and uncovered in the days to come. *Bistari*.

Here Comes The Boom!

WHEN I FIND MYSELF IN A DREAMLESS STATE OR A PLACE OF DRIP-DROP DREAMS, I PLAY IT SAFE.

I hide and isolate myself from my trusted tribe, those who inspire and support me. Fear takes hold and courage—whoosh—is gone.

Day-to-day endeavors become laborious and heavy. Work is hard—too hard. I might be doing lots of good, but the *DOing* is forced and compressed. It seems there is not enough of me, of time, of anything.

Can you relate? Have you forgotten to dream or are you dreaming small—drip-drop—dreams? Are you too often alone and isolated? Is the everyday *DOing* in your life just plain hard? Have you been playing it a bit too safe, or have you been afraid to move in any direction?

If you have been living in a less-than-you way, step out of the shadows, and drop your strenuous doing. C'mon out. It's time for some good news. Are you ready? Here comes the *boom*!

The time is now to effortlessly kindle your dreams. You need not try harder. You only need to patiently and fervently trust that where you are is just right. Each and every step of the way, you have been mysteriously and dynamically prepared by your own heart, by life, and by those around you to be where you are right now on this *jOURney*.

If you are living on the fumes of hope, I promise that bigger dreams than you could think to ask for or imagine are yours. You have a powerful purpose on the planet and others who are waiting for you to join in the fun with them. The dreams and your purpose are the kindling—they are ready to be ignited, even though you may not see or fully understand them yet.

Over time, fueled by your destiny and those who support you, you will begin to think, speak, and act differently. Although fear doesn't go away, it will no longer stop you from taking the next step—at least, not for long. You will stop hiding; you will pick yourself up (or get pulled up by others), step out of the safe shadows, take a deep breath, and march on. You will be beckoned to speak and *emPOWERed* to bust out of a dreamless or drip-drop state into a dreaming bigger one. When these things happen, there will be no going back. *You won't want to.* Life will be a riveting adventure that you love.

> Dream big.
> Start small.
> But most of all, start.
> -Simon Sinek

For me, it has been about audaciously trusting and living into this truth in my everyday life, particularly in the days of doubt and moments of battling to believe there are breathtaking dreams in me and a one-of-a-kind purpose that will make the world a bit brighter. Tending to the drip-drop dreams has led, step-by-step, day-by-day, leap-by-leap, to some oceanic ones. At those times, things that initially appeared impossible began to happen—and *Bam!* Another dream was kindled, becoming real and more glorious than I'd ever imagined.

Wherever you are, whatever you're doing, imagine what your dream looks and feels like. Start from where you are ... whether in the carpool line; at home doing laundry; at your office or shop; driving a cab, tuck-tuck, or rickshaw; making pasta, samosas, posh, or arapas; caring for young children or elderly parents; entering college or starting a new career in the middle of life; loving work or hating it; hopeful or hopeless. No matter where you are in this moment, your dreams and desires are being lit up. Get ready for the *Boom!* of what will happen as it kindles.

▶ 1 *Be Still (surrender)*

Surrender. Silence. Stillness.
Breathe. Take some long, deep breaths. Relax your
muscles from the tip of your head to your toes.
Enjoy being, just being, for a few moments.
Stop moving, racing, thinking, planning.
Stay here for ten seconds or ten minutes.

ponder (go deeper)

Listen to the song, "Go," sung by Sandra McCracken.
Fellas, swap out the female pronouns for your own ... you
are part of this story too. Imagine the places to which you
are being drawn, the parts of life that are becoming more
clear, and consider if you are ready to *go*. Listen for and
watch the doubt and the noises becoming quieter. *Ahh.*
Write about what comes to you.

What phrases or images struck you as you read this
chapter? These are crumbs and clues for the road ahead,
meant just for you. Sit with them. Explore what connections there are in your life today to these morsels of
insight.

• •

What comes to you as you consider your *drip-drop* dreams and desires? Do you see a small dream that might grow, bit by bit, into a bigger, perhaps even an oceanic, one? Have you been living in a smaller-than-is-really-you vision of yourself? Where in your life, in your dreams, would you like a *Boom!* of ignition?

Engage (commit)

A nudge. Do one thing today for the pure joy of it, with no anticipated outcome other than your enjoyment. Whether it's what you eat, listen to, watch, do, or who you spend time with … this is all about connecting with your heart's desire, your longing in an everyday way. *This* is kindling your dreams.

Now, it's your turn. What or who are you beckoned to *commit to, connect with,* or *create*—whether in small or big ways?

Share something from this PoP with someone you trust.

BE BOLD. BE BRAVE. BE YOU.

unstoppable

You are destined for more than
you can be and do on your own.
Individually, you are extraordinary,
with great capacity and power.
Yup, you rock.

And ... there's more.
When you open your heart and mind
to the people around you,
to those in your mighty human family
—strangers and friends alike—
you will discover possibilities,
joy, and strength
in surprising places.

Humbly and WHOLEheartedly,
see and welcome others into your story,
and invite them to share their own.

Together, life is better.
Infinitely more is possible.
You—we—are unstoppable.

Vital Tribe

WHETHER I FEEL GOOD OR BAD, STRONG OR WEAK, ON TOP OF THE WORLD, OR AT ROCK BOTTOM, I HAVE EXPERIENCED OVER AND OVER WHAT HAPPENS WITH MY TRIBE. IT'S MAGIC.

It's breathtaking. It's real. It's game-changing and difference-making. This tribe I speak of is composed of a vital three-part collective without whom I cannot imagine navigating life—from dealing with the day-to-day minutia, to epic leaps of courage, to going after big dreams. Each one matters greatly.

First and foremost is my relationship with the Sacred, who is with me—present, persistent, and pervading—in every single bit of life, no matter the content or context: relational or vocational, healing or heartbreaking, messy or clear, hopeful or hopeless. Everything begins, is sustained, and ends here in my life. The second element of my tribe is my trusted soul friends, with whom I grow and to whom I am committed to share all of me … my highest hopes and greatest foibles. The third aspect is comprised of those I don't yet know—"strangers," for now—in my human family, but with whom there is a growing sense of being more inextricably interconnected each day. They are the ones who inspire and fuel my purpose and passions on a daily basis.

I know I am never alone—never have been and never will be. For me, this not-being-alone piece is about my human community of brothers and sisters and of the Sacred. I need both. The seasons in which I have stopped cultivating my relationship with either have been the darkest of my life. But together—in a vibrant, raw and real, open connection with the Sacred and community—this is where I have found limitless joy, freedom, innovation, power, wonder, beauty, hope, love, and value. Over and over ... without boundaries and without fail.

Each part of this collective of my tribe is vital to the other. They each fuel my energies to engage with the other. They each adjust the aperture of my vision for the other. They each keep me coming back to sit with, learn from, listen to, and speak with the other. They each open me up to see my path and purpose more clearly.

My friend, I believe, with all my heart, that this is true for you, too.

Your purpose on the planet—big or small in impact, local or global—is not about carving something out alone; it only happens with others. The tribe you want to travel with through life may look very different from mine. No doubt, your collective will have a unique flavor. But, no matter how it looks, it must not be a tribe of one, in which you are doing life by yourself.

Your plane will be grounded and your wheels harnessed to the cement if you try to go it alone. To those of you who think you can fly solo, I double-dog-dare you to see where this journey with others takes you. The good news about this adventure is that with a community of support, you will create a richer, more vibrant support system than ever that will *enCOURAGE* you to *be bold, be brave, and be you.*

Although you may be more inclined to move through your days in a privately personal and introverted manner, this goes beyond personality types and tendencies. The need to move through life in a more communal manner truly is a "must" for all of us. Self-help is a crock. It is elusive. It never lives up to its promises for a life that is flourishing and *good*. Going it alone is barely feasible even in seasons of ease, where there are no great highs or lows. And big leaps, even the joyful and mighty ones, require being bolstered by others for perspective, energy, or encouragement that you can't access on your own.

Regardless of how capable or weak you feel, you need a few trustworthy others to remind you what is true, what is good, what is *hopeFULL*, to pull you up off the ground when you fall, and to cheer you on when you have been boldly and bravely you. This is not about having a full social calendar. Even within a life plentiful with people, full-to-the-brim with relationships of family, work, and friends, you can feel alone. There is a balance that must be struck. Staying too busy or re-maining for too long in isolation each has the potential to expand the craters of questions and pain within and around you.

> My community, my trusted tribe, helps me to see life —to see myself— differently.
> -Godee Musangu, *kula* sister

Instead, this way of creative and committed living sets many mo-mentous things in motion. A fierce certainty about your unique and unstoppable purpose on the planet will—either in a *bistari* way or in a flash—come more clearly into focus. It is here that you will find your *why* in life, in a bigger way than ever before. It is here that you will discover more of your own story, more of what truly matters to you. What before seemed impossible will begin to capture your eye, now palpable with possibility. More becomes *doABLE*. Conversations happen and connections are fostered that will change you. Opportunities will arise to share your story in a more amplified way. When you do, your community will hear and celebrate your voice and your unique ways of living life. You will be open to their perspective about blind spots in your life that have made life—until now—unclear and challenging. You are freer to be *you* in the company of and in conversation with this dynamic collective.

These notions may strike you as a mixed bag of good and bad news. Part of you may be in agreement and part of you may contest it. You may be nodding your head, having experienced these ideas to be true. Or you may be triggered at the suggestion that there are things you cannot do on your own. I get it. There have been times when I've wrestled with this notion of a tribe, other times when I've explored it, and still others when I've basked in the interdependence of this collective. I see it now: all of it—the wrestling, the exploring, the crafting—has led me to a stunning reality of a life today that *glitters with gifts* given by this mysterious tribe.

This is yet another moment when I wish we could be sitting together, sharing thoughts and feelings about such a vital tribe. Wherever you are on this trajectory, I invite you to commit to the idea that there is something to be explored, that there may be a gleaming gift waiting for you, and that such a tribe may open you up to see and live your unstoppable and one-of-a-kind purpose on the planet like never before.

Surrounded by Sacred

THERE ARE MANY WAYS TO CONNECT WITH THE SACRED ... THAT SOMETHING OR SOMEONE GREATER THAN YOU.

It's stunning to see the diverse ways in which people cultivate this part of themselves—within and outside of religious communities; in buildings of worship and outside in nature; practicing yoga, prayer, and meditation; and on and on.

We have golden opportunities throughout much of life to learn from and listen to the varied ways others foster their spiritual journeys. Transparency about what matters to each of us, and being open to the same in others, can create magnificent bridges of connection. These bridges are particularly paramount in places of division—whether within our intimate relationships or in our local neighborhoods or distant countries.

Being a part of this prismatic variety in all of life is one of my great loves. And yet, truth be told, were it not for the voice of Bill, an elder in my community, I would have inadvertently left out a big piece of my story—a basic part of who I am. But he didn't miss it. It was clear as day to him. As he read an early draft of this book, he noticed a gaping hole. In a conversation one morning, he asked me why I was only telling part of my story.

As we talked, I realized that I was hiding. I hid because I worried that the moment I shared a personal perspective about spirituality that you found different, foolish, or unfamiliar, you would set aside this book and not reopen it. I feared that if I wholeheartedly spoke to the essential spiritual roots of my heart—of myself—you'd distrust or dislike me. I thought that this part of my story would disqualify me in your eyes. My wise elder, Bill, saw me hiding in the shadows and nudged me to *c'mon out* and tell the truth. *To be bold. To be brave. To be me.*

So, my friend, in order to be transparent, so that you know exactly where I am in terms of the Sacred, here is what is true for me, in a raw and real, nothin'-to-hide sort of a way. God is the warp and woof of me and has always been my heartbeat, my Tour Guide in life—whether in moments of pain or joy, in times of knowing or uncertainty, when feeling like a rock star or at rock bottom. In an always-steady flow of conversation with God, I have been directed away from many-a-dead-end and revived when my head was hanging low. I feel that I bring joy to God's heart just by being alive. I see and experience God everywhere … in all people and places. God is the Source of Love that fuels and frees me in my life and is the reason I am living and breathing today. This Love changes everything—this Love has changed me.

> Transparency about what matters to each of us, and being open to the same in others, can create magnificent bridges of connection.

God is the ultimate Source of everything good in my life. The starting point for my connection with God is Jesus. This has been true for me ever since I was a little girl. This relationship has seen me through rough days, has *emBOLDened* me to see and offer the gifts I have that will make the world better, and has encouraged me to be more uniquely and securely me. I converse with Jesus as my ever-present brother as I go about my days, hearing His voice speaking whatever I most need to hear every single time I listen.

My words for the Sacred are most often God and Jesus. Thus, when I speak of my personal life, I will use these words, my "first language" in my spiritual journey. But when it is about a collective spiritual journey, I will use the words Sacred and Spirit.

By virtue of the diversity in our human experience, I understand that these words or even the capitalization of the words will not work for everyone. In order to personalize the Sacred for yourself, freely substitute the words I use with the word or phrase that takes you most deeply into your spiritual connection. This, I hope, will keep us walking, growing, and *jOURneying* together in the days to come.

What held me back from wholly sharing my story was my fear of the divisiveness that can occur when we don't use the same name for or contest the very existence of the Sacred. But, I fully believe that the time is now to create a community *with arms flung open* to each other, in places of similarity *and* difference, whether we share the same language or not.

Dear friend, we've hit another moment—this one, a big and personal one—in which I wish, with all my heart, that I could be sitting with you to hear your story, to listen to what resonates with you, and what doesn't, around spirituality and a relationship with the Sacred. To listen to the joy, solace, or pain that this touches in your life. To hear how the Spirit intersects (or doesn't) with your day-to-day comings and goings.

Although we cannot be together, I imagine, think about, and am sending good juju your way this day. May whatever you most need in this moment be yours: love, courage, peace, a bit of lightness, hope, and more to you, dear one.

Trusted Soul Friends

**FOR ME, THERE IS NO DOUBT, NOT ONE SINGLE DOUBT,
THAT I COULD NOT HAVE DONE MUCH OF ANYTHING
ON MY LIFE'S JOURNEY WITHOUT MY TRUSTED SOUL FRIENDS.**

**They spur me to keep going every single day.
There have been many times I would have been
trapped in the muck and mire of fear, hurt, or
discouragement without these trusted soul friends.**

The other day, I had one such experience. I was in one of those
oh-so-common human moments, in which I was terribly disheart-
ened and held in the grip of anxiety. I had crawled under a rock,
so to speak, because I wanted to hide and be invisible for a
while.

In the midst of this bugger of a time, Rachael Jayne, a wise sister,
sidled up to me, joining me under that rock. She reminded me
about what I had forgotten. She nudged me to recall the big truths
of who I am and to see the beauty in my moment of pain. She
asked me to consider long-standing patterns of hiding, of staying
small and quiet. I knew, even as she spoke the words, that she
was speaking truth. Rachael Jayne challenged me to do something to break this pattern.

As luck (or fate) would have it, I was at a speaker's training conference with a stage (gulp!), so during an *open mic* moment directly
following our conversation, I brazenly and uncharacteristically did
something new. I stood up, took the microphone, and shared the

raw and the real in my story. Right then and there. I shared my history of hiding too often. Of whispering too much. Of being syrupy-sweet instead of audaciously authentic. It was terrifying. And amazing. And it freed me, a bit more, from the chains of smaller-than-me ways of life.

As I pondered this experience, an epiphany kindled: *The story that's in me to live, I cannot write into existence alone.* To be sure, it would have been much more comfortable to have chosen to *learn* this lesson in a far more private manner … say, in the pages of my journal or in quiet times of contemplation and prayer. Yet, although those times of solitude have riches of their own, there is an essential element of expansive growth that is *kindled in the company of others.*

> The time is now to create a community with arms flung open to each other, in places of similarity and difference, whether we share the same language or not.

On that day, as on many other days, I need others to *reflect* back to me what they see, to *beckon* me to places I'm not quite sure I can go alone, to *listen* to what matters to me, to *witness* my bold (albeit trembling) moments of voicing my story.

These things—the reflecting, beckoning, and listening—are some of the great invitations to each of us, with one another as a tribe. This is exactly what happened at the birthday party this year for a dear friend Kathleen.

We feasted on platters of steaming Indian and Nepali food, toasted Kathleen's *beautyFULL* life thus far, and blessed her new year to come. After dinner, under the twinkling stars on a warm summer night, she reflected on the change in her life over the previous year:

"For the first time in my life—I belong somewhere. Until now, I have wandered. But, now I am at home and I have hope because I have people with whom I feel I am valuable. Always. It is life-changing. What has surprised me is that I still have someplace I belong on my bad days. Even when I have nothing to offer, I do not feel less than you guys. So, even when I am a mess, I am accepted. I am convinced that we cannot be fully human if we are not part of community where we belong. This belonging inspires me to do something. I am fired up to do something, to share this same hope and experience of belonging with others."

We wildly cheered her on, heartily clinking our wine glasses for this full-to-the-brim *goodness*. We were even more exuberant in our cheers, in part, because we have been a part of her story. We know that the *goodness* of this season hasn't always been so. For Kathleen, this is a new reality in her life. In years past, she did all the *right things*. She read books, went to counseling, took classes, and explored career options. She was doing everything she knew to do. But she was doing it alone. And she was lost in her *aloneness*.

The epic change happened for her as she began surrounding herself with us, a circle of five trusted sister-friends. We have each committed to unabashedly and truly share our struggles, along with our emerging hopes, with one another. There is an ancient Sanskrit word, *kula*, which means "community of the heart." Well, this is the essence of the *kula*. Here, in our *kula* of trusted soul sisters, she began to confidently share more bits of her story and her glittering gifts, and a fresh energy emerged in her everyday life. Before long, we saw her reach out from our safe circle, and she began volunteering her time with a few organizations that are close to her heart. She offered what she had to give with joy and ease, out of the overflow and fuel of belonging and living *BEloved* with her sisters.

We see it. She *is* different. She has been strengthened, mightily so, by her circle of soul sisters. She is more radiant, powerful, and visionary in every arena of her life: within herself, in her marriage, in motherhood, at work, and in her vision to serve using her unique gifts. She is rocking and loving this *kula* life.

We all need this. You, too, need a trusted few with whom you can be you— to laugh or cry, to rock life or flail, to be loud or be quiet. These are the ones with whom you are able to be real, together. Living a life of raw and real interconnection makes life better.

> I am convinced that we cannot be fully human if we are not part of a community where we belong.
> -Kathleen Vigil
> *kula* sister

Shared Humanity

ENLARGING YOUR VISION FOR AND COMMITMENT TO THOSE "STRANGERS" IN YOUR COLOSSAL AND COMMON HUMAN FAMILY CHANGES YOUR THOUGHTS, ACTIONS, AND HEART ... SOMETIMES IN EVERYDAY AND SMALL WAYS AND AT OTHER TIMES IN LIFE-ALTERING EPIC WAYS.

It is here that a sense of belonging to, *comPASSIONate* attention, and responsibility for one another grows—whether with those unknown or known to you.

Can you imagine the mighty movement that would be unleashed if, one by one, we each opened up our minds and hearts to those we don't yet know, love, or call friend or family? This simple and humble opening cultivates the conditions for change in our conversations, choices, and actions.

How might it alter our engagement with people portrayed in the news and on social media if we saw them not as *strangers* but as people connected to us? Might it result in lessening judgment, fear, and distrust? I have a hunch the answer is yes. It has done so in my life. And I see it happening all over the world in both little and large ways.

Pope Francis spoke with simple and powerful wisdom about this inextricable interconnection in a TED talk during the annual TED Conference in Vancouver on April 25, 2017, "Why the Only Future Worth Building Includes Everyone:"

How wonderful would it be, while we discover faraway planets, to rediscover the needs of the brothers and sisters orbiting around us.

All it takes is for one person to stop and help, and change the lives of people around us, turning a small ripple into a revolution …

Through the darkness of today's conflicts, each and every one of us can become a bright candle, a reminder that light will overcome darkness, and never the other way around.

Arms Flung Open

HAVE YOU BEEN TEMPTED TO LOP OFF LIMBS OR HIDE BIG PARTS OF YOURSELF, BELIEVING THAT IF YOU SHARE THAT ASPECT OF WHO YOU ARE, PEOPLE WILL BE UNABLE TO HANDLE IT AND WILL TURN AWAY?

Have you lived scared that you will be misunderstood and judged if you truthfully speak about that thing? Take a look at the diversity that exists between you and those nearest and dearest to you: your spouse, kids, family, or closest friends.

Are there parts of you that you conceal from those closest to you? Are there differences that dangerously divide? If so, you have company. I initially concealed the fullness of my love story with God from you. But, do you know what? There's more. Truth be told, my hiding and lopping off essential bits of myself has also been present in another love story in my life, smack dab in the middle of my marriage.

My husband and I are very diverse, shall I say, in both little *and* big matters: I like the heat high; he likes it low. I love to hop on an airplane to go ... well, really, anywhere; he hates most every-thing about airplanes and travel. I am drawn toward simplicity; he loves luxury. I am inclined to be exceedingly serious; he is wildly comedic. I thrive within a vibrant community life; he would choose to live in a cave of quiet. This list goes on and on.

And the ways he does things. Is. Just. So. *Different.*

When we first met twenty-five years ago, these very contrary ways of doing things wooed and captivated me. I was intrigued and longed for some of his yin to be part of my yang. He became one of my best friends ... and then the *spark* of love was kindled. In those early days of dating, my, how these differences glittered! They were beautiful. They were what drew us toward each other and seemed to be the glue that held us together. I basked in his glow and I fell head-over-heals-in-love. Then, I asked him to marry me.

Throughout the years of our mysterious life as wife and husband, there have been seasons in which these differences morphed into things that felt more uncomfortable than beautiful, more dissonant than harmonious. There have been days in which we lived divided by the very things that initially drew us to say "I do."

There were days I endeavored to try and change him to be more like me, or I contorted myself to be more like him, trying to reconcile the disparities by cultivating sameness. (*That* didn't work, at all.) There were days when the differences were all I could see, and at those times, they expanded and caused greater division, often quietly underground. (*That* was disastrous.) The more I focused on and lamented the problems related to our differences, the bigger they grew. In those days, I nearly allowed, unknowingly passive and foolishly unwitting, this diversity to tear and pull us apart.

But in it all—even in the most dark and disappointing, grueling and gloomy days—a flame flickered. Hope kindled. In the midst of raw and real conversations with God, with my man, Bran, and with others in my trusted tribe, a spark of light continued to glow. *Ahh.* Day-by-day, step-by-step, in these times of pausing and listening, in the midst of the struggle, I began to see anew. I began to see gems glittering in the dissimilarities. I began to celebrate the very things that I used to lament.

For good reason. There is much to celebrate and much that glitters. This man is stunning. His generosity is unparalleled. He is one of the greatest everyday philanthropists I've ever known. He is the *straw that stirs the drink*, bringing lightness, laughter, and pure joy wherever he is—whether at an intimate family gathering, at a party of friends, or at his work. He is so very wise, with clarity that seems both effortless and fierce. He sees a path forward in a blink. Once he makes a plan, he sticks with it through thick and thin. He is a bedrock of stability and security. He is unwavering.

Life is better with this man *because* of the ways he is and does *different*. They are what make me cock my head in wonder and my eyes sparkle with pride at the ease with which he navigates terrains that seem virtually impossible to me.

This is all true. *It always has been true.* And yet, also true, is that sometimes I didn't have eyes to see the gifts—our *secret ingredients*—within the differences themselves.

A few years ago, it was discovered that the sturdiest segments of the iconic Great Wall of China have been held together with mortar composed of a very ordinary and organic *secret ingredient*: sticky rice. Mortar is the paste used to bind together and seal gaps between building blocks such as stones and bricks. Scientists have discovered that sticky rice flour was added to other standard mortar ingredients in certain sections of the Great Wall. Yes, sticky rice mortar, composed of one of the most *everyday* ingredients in China, is now being described as one of the *great technical innovations of its time*.

For 1,500 years, this secret ingredient—the simple and common material of sticky rice—has quietly proven its durability, holding the stones of the wall together through earthquakes, floods, and other natural disasters. This organic ingredient is said to be remarkably *compatible* with other standard mortar ingredients. Researchers have discovered that the segments of the wall where *ordinary* sticky rice flour was utilized in its mortar have stood the test of time with *extraordinary* mechanical strength and stability.

> But in it all—even in the most dark and disappointing, grueling and gloomy days—a flame flickered. Hope kindled.

And so it is with Brandon and me. The ways in which we are different have become our *secret ingredients* of surprising compatibility, an integral part of the glue, the mortar, and the strongest stuff binding us together. I marvel at the elements of strength and stability in our marriage. It is breathtaking to consider, because it's a pure miracle. I share this not as a sappy, annoying marriage affirmation, but as a surprising and awesome wonder.

The way he cheers me on is also astonishing. It is astonishing because it emanates from the lips of the one *more different* from me than most. Through this, he has been a demonstration—in the humdrum and ordinariness of marriage—of a way to *live large and love big* in the midst of *otherness*. And, yes. Without a doubt and to be crystal clear: in the midst of all of this wonder and *awesomeness*, it remains a commitment that requires me to be attentive, humble, and real … every day. I am still a student learning what loving and being loved looks like, each and every day, with this marvel of a man.

My friend, how about you? When it comes to important and deep parts within you, in areas such as spirituality and relation- ships, it is common and oh, so human, to be afraid that the dif- ferences will divide. It may be terrifying to share with others what really matters to you. You may fear what will happen if others really see you—if they catch a glimpse of what you believe in or love, of what matters most or least to you, and to what you are committed.

And you're right. It happens. All the time. Lashing out, exclusion, judgment, competition, gossip, and petty grievances are prevalent realities in the world. Whether between friends or strangers, it can hurt … a lot. It can close us off to each other.

But another way—*a free and brave way*—beckons.

Explore, experiment, and experience what happens when you walk more often open to those who seem uncomfortably *unlike* you. Living with your *arms flung open* bridges *you with others*. This is a radical resolution, a brave way, to be sure. This is a cou- rageous commitment that is even more important—and perhaps difficult—when the dissimilarities are vast.

2 Be Still (surrender)

My friend, take this time,
whether it's ten seconds or ten minutes.
Be here. Be open. Be still.

ponder (go deeper)

Imagine being on the highest point of The Great Wall of China, at 5,033 feet, nearly a mile above sea level, when you listen to this rousing song by Imagine Dragons, "On Top of the World." *Ponder* and write about the words or phrases you love and the rhythms that get your toes tappin'.

What parts of yourself do you hide, fearing judgment or disconnection from people closest to you? Are they related to your political views, spiritual beliefs, the highs or lows of your bank account ... or to how you look, how you feel, or something else?

Consider and/or write about two different experiences. One in which you shared yourself with another and it resulted in exclusion or separation, and one in which there was a profound exchange and a palpable sense of coming together. What elements do you see that set up the different outcomes? Be descriptive about the where, who, when, and how of it.

How might you invite others to be more real and raw, wholeheartedly sharing themselves with you? In what ways might this shift the ways in which you think about differences in the bigger community of your mighty human family?

Engage (commit)

A nudge. Find one time today to either share a raw and real part of yourself with another—a part you typically hide from others—and/or welcome the same in another. Consider having this interaction with someone near and dear to you, someone with whom you are very intimate, but from whom you hide a part of yourself.

Now, it's your turn. What or who are you beckoned to *commit to, connect with,* or *create*—whether in small or big ways?

Share something from this PoP with someone you trust.

BE BOLD. BE BRAVE. BE YOU.

practices & perspectives

This jOURney is a simple one
of sharing and exchanging a few seeds of stories,
watching for tendrils of what grows in you
and working it into the soil of your everyday life.

The practices and perspectives that follow
will kindle, awaken, and illuminate
more of what matters most to you,
lighting you up with a clearer vision than ever
for your purpose on the planet.

Who knows, maybe this excitement
will be felt by those closest to you
or begin to take shape to connect
with the lives of those
in far-flung neighborhoods in the world.

Simple & Small

THE SMALL AND SIMPLE CAN INDEED BE SIGNIFICANT. THEY CAN BE MORE THAN ENOUGH.

This *jOURney* is not necessarily about making big changes. It is about humbly committing to the value of doing small things, of reaching out to others with great love.

One of my dear soul friends, Raquel, is a momma of triplet boys who are two years old and to a little girl who is five. Life is, shall we say, *full*. In the midst of the daily work of caring for her brood of little ones, she has created a sanctuary by surrounding her young tribe with music, feasting, books, prayer, and laughter.

Raquel is fiercely committed to intentionally planting seeds of kindness, beauty, faith, and joy in her children, each and every day. To that end, Raquel asks her children to do an act of love for their family each day *that goes unnoticed*. Raquel is beckoning her little ones to practice quietly simple service. It is woven into the everyday … *humbly performed without fanfare*.

My goodness. Can you imagine if we each took on Raquel's invitation and committed to offering one daily act of love that goes unnoticed? Quietly simple service like this could light up the world.

My wise and beloved Aunt Deby recently spoke about her process of considering and committing to small acts with this very spirit of freedom and simplicity. She had been a part of a conversation with some of our Seeds of Exchange changemakers who

> This *jOURney* is not necessarily about making big changes. It is about humbly committing to the value of doing small things, of reaching out to others with great love.

are passionately working to fight the great global injustice of human trafficking. What struck her during this dialogue about an epic global challenge was a quiet and powerful nudge in her heart to respond with simplicity. *To simply respond.*

She didn't have the answers or the ability to *fix* this complex challenge, but she wanted to do her little part. This permission to do a little thing, knowing that it wouldn't solve the problem, opened up something in my Aunt Deby. In that moment, she committed to act, by saying, "I tend to always think I have to do the big thing. The idea of a small action fosters in me the desire and commitment to do something. I will simply show up and do my part."

Delta Donohue, a soul sister and author of *The First Taste Belongs to the Gods*, shared a story from her life, one that is rooted in the reality that though this journey is simple, it isn't always convenient. It may even cost you, asking you to give what you have ... asking you to give *yourself*.

It was a blazing hot day this past summer when her townhouse complex was being repainted. One morning, Delta noticed the painters outside her window, and she smiled and went outside to say hello, carrying some water and a plate of cookies. The men gratefully responded, *"Gracias!"* (Spanish for "Thank you!")

Delta has a full-to-the-brim life. When she looked out her window and saw the men sweating and painting, she was busy. It wasn't convenient or during a period in her life when she felt she had an excess amount of time to give to the men. She was in the midst of publishing her first book, collaborating to expand a social enterprise with a visionary friend in India, working in a school teaching English as a Second Language (ESL), and committed to serving and loving her family in their day-to-day needs.

She didn't know what would happen as a result of her small act of love. But, as Delta simply offered and served these *strangers* water and cookies, they exchanged names, and shared some brief stories about family and work. The painters were intrigued by her work as an ESL educator.

Walking out her door to say hello, sharing some food, and discovering one another's names led to a bold question: "*¿Podrías enseñarnos inglés?*" ("Could you teach us English?") Although she had more than enough in her life to tend to, she was eager and open to respond to their request. Delta reached out to the owner of the painting company, proposing that she teach the men English during their breaks. She asked if he would be willing to allow them a longer break and pay for the class. He said no, it wasn't possible.

Embedded in this story's "no" lies another gold nugget for us. Delta's story didn't have the outcome she and the men hoped for at that time, but we know the story is not over. Although we may never be able to measure the impact of her offer of water, of exchanging names, of exploring the possibilities of learning English together, of sharing life together during a few moments on those hot summer days, it

> Small things with great, great love.
> This is compassion.
> Compassion is not pity.
> Pity is your pain in my heart. It just sits there.
> It heals nothing.
> But compassion.
> Compassion is your pain in my heart and back out through my hands.
> -Glennon Doyle Melton, Momastery blog

was clear from their exchange that Delta and the men were each touched by the other.

Sometimes we may see the ripples of these little, often-invisible acts, and at other times, we won't. Perhaps this is one of the gifts of these humble *DOings*: to be free from the need to know where they will lead, but to simply serve. To *be love*.

Ebbing & Flowing

IMAGINE, FOR A MOMENT, THAT YOU ARE SITTING NEAR THE WATER'S EDGE, TOES AND FINGERS MOVING IN THE SAND.

The sunrise warms your face. Ocean breezes tickle your skin. Birds greet the morning with lilting songs. You smile and close your eyes.

You listen to the waves in their dance as they roll forward and rhythmically fall back into themselves. The sound calms. Your breath deepens and your heartbeat slows. *Ahh.*

Now, in your imagination, as you watch and listen to the ebb and flow of the ocean, consider the epic catastrophe of an ocean that moves with an unceasing ebb or flow. The surging energy with no release or a never-ending ebb would be a natural disaster.

It's the same for you. Too much of either of these movements is unbalanced and unsustainable. It sets the stage for disaster. Neither the ocean nor you can function for long without the regular, rhythmic patterns of *both* ebb and flow, quiet and action, solitude and community, self-care and service.

Ebb living for too long can become a place of hiding, withdrawing, and isolation. It can make for too many low-energy days. You were meant for more. You were meant to *do*, to *flow*, energized by expressing your unique purpose on the planet. So, if you find yourself in never-ending ebb living, it may be time to kindle and spark those dreams, say yes more often, and spread your arms a bit wider.

Conversely, continuous flow living can find you exhausted and overwhelmed in the unending pressure to do more and the relentless push to power forward. You may find yourself in the grueling surge of never-ending work and incessant to-do lists. *Oof.* How well I know this place of being tired to the bone, with no rest in sight, a sense of isolation in the clamoring and crushing needs of many. If this is you, it may be time to cultivate a rhythm of *bistari* (that beautiful Nepali word for "slowly"), of intentional and regular pauses. To be still. To be quiet. To rest.

> A silent heart is a loving heart,
> and a loving heart
> is a hospice to the world ...
> My life of service and love
> to my fellow man
> is simply the echo
> of this silence and solitude ...
> Now I become as one on fire
> with love of Him and all
> humanity.
> -Catherine Doherty Poustinia

Finding a way regularly punctuated with *bistari*, with ebb, will fuel you with wisdom for the moments of coursing action and swelling service that follow. Each day, a sense of palpable knowing and clarity about what is your thing to do—or not—will be yours.

This intentional and rhythmic movement of ebb and flow living will change you. Your senses will be tuned to when you need to re-center by moving more towards one or the other. Your fuel tank will be on empty less often. You will dream big and love bigger. More often, your arms will be merrily flung open to your human family. Your vision will be expanded to embrace a life of inspired doing *and* the nourishing stillness of being.

Garden Life

LIVING IN COLORADO, THERE ARE FOUR DISTINCTIVELY DIFFERENT SEASONS.

Fall is jaw-dropping. It's the season when the aspen tree leaves turn golden colors and vibrant red maple leaves fall to the ground, waiting to be raked up and played in by giggling young ones.

Winters are beautiful in their simplicity. They are exceedingly stark, the sun sits low, and the light disappears early. While nature's appearance is more stark than flourishing, more barren than vibrant, there are plentiful gifts that are fostered in this season. Often, we move a bit more slowly, go to bed a bit earlier, and cozy up together with candlelight and steaming cups of tea.

There are times when life seems to move so very *bistari*—slowly. Growth takes time, and it cannot be rushed or forced. And growth can be nearly imperceptible while life is being strengthened or prepared underground. When I see this in my garden and in nature around me, when I connect it to my life, it encourages me to relax and *enJOY* the moments of less-than-visible and seemingly slow growth.

Spring reminds me of the growth that was happening underground during the dark and cold days, as the bulbs peak above the soil and the trees bud and leaf out. As summer approaches, kids are gleeful at the hiatus of school days. Summer days are hot and long, full of playful, vibrant energy.

One recent summer day, my garden spoke to me. Deeply. It beckoned me to come and see, to *be still* and *ponder*. As I did, I saw it clearly. There was far too much growing too close together. At this rate, the plants would start to choke out each other and no longer be able to thrive. The garden needed to be thinned in order to allow each plant ample room—without having to compete with other plants. The same is true for us. At times, there is a need for attentive space-making to cultivate conditions for vibrant growth.

> Above all, trust in the slow work of God. We are quite naturally impatient in everything to reach the end without delay. We should like to skip the intermediate stages. We are impatient of being on the way to something unknown, something new.
> -Teilhard de Chardin excerpt of prayer-poem, "Patient Trust"

A garden and nature's seasons remind us that life and growth are happening, with each season offering distinct ways to move through our days.

Letting Go & Wading In

I'VE DISCOVERED I CAN LOVE AND SERVE MOST WHOLEHEARTEDLY AND DEEPLY WHEN I RELEASE ANY SENSE THAT FIXING THE PROBLEM IS ENTIRELY UP TO ME.

Most often, the solution is beyond me. That's the truth 99.9% of the time.

This *letting go* is humbling and freeing. And, I've come to see that letting go is often accompanied by a nudge to *wade in*.

This *letting go* is humbling and freeing. And, I've come to see that *letting go* is often accompanied by a nudge to *wade in*. This is another one of those complementary both/ands of soulful living. These opposites are often connected. Watch for it in the days to come.

Wading in is about compassionately getting close to one who is struggling—seeing, listening, and *being with* them. It most often involves a time to *be still* and *ponder*, "What is my part, if any?" It may be followed by a palpable sense that it is time for me to *participate* and *do* something, but to do so free of the sense that it's my job to fix the person or the problem. Again: most everything is greater than my capacity to solve.

> Letting go beckons. It calls us to wade in and tend to those we are destined to serve and enCOURAGES us to light up the world with our purpose on the planet.

I have also come to know that in order to *wade in* and be with people throughout the sorrows of life, I must develop a regular, rhythmic practice of humbly letting go. I believe, with all my heart, that the same is true for you. Whether the one you love is a toddler teething, a teenager individuating, a spouse isolating, a news story highlighting the broken and terrifying, *let go* ... and *wade in*.

Letting go frees. It humbles. It is peaceful. It is an exhale. It buffers us from the illusion that we can or ought to try to save the world and protects us from being burned out by the burden of overzealousness.

Letting go beckons. It calls us to wade in and tend to those we are destined to serve and *enCOURAGES* us to light up the world with our purpose on the planet.

Robust Rhythms

MY LITTLE MAN, MICAH, IS THE KING OF COZY.

He loves to linger snug-as-a-bug-in-a-rug in his bed, cuddling with and surrounded by fifty-three (yes, we've counted them) stuffed animals of various sizes. He's a romantic fella, is all about the comfy and moving in that *bistari* way.

That is, until it comes to one of his great passions in life: "screen time." This love of his motivates him to set his alarm earlier than required on school mornings, to make his way out of his cozy stuffed-animal-stuffed-bed, and briskly get ready for the day, so that he has the joy of playing games before breakfast. His desire compels and propels him to move differently on school mornings.

On one morning, he found he'd forgotten to plug in his iPod before he went to bed the night before. When he picked it up, it was low on battery power, and there was no juice left in the device for him to play. In no time, he found a portable charger, plugged it in, and started playing.

Micah's low-battery-device morning and his deeply compelling desire to play games before school got me thinking about the ways we grownups deal with our battery power. I am curious: What's your battery level right now? When was the last time your batteries felt fully charged? Do you have ways to fuel up when you're on the go and running low on energy? This nudge is intended to be deeply practical, giving you the opportunity to consider the ways you might regularly renew and fuel yourself for the rigors of daily life.

One place to start this living full-to-the-brim with a fully charged battery is by cultivating a lens that looks for the good and sees the plenty *now*. Gratitude is one of the most sustainable and simple ways to recharge and stay charged. It is talked about within many spiritual and personal growth traditions so pervasively that sometimes our hearts and minds can miss the infinite gift it offers to change the very texture of life.

Maybe you're thinking, *Yeah, yeah, grateFULLness is important. I know it is. But, right now, life is hard ... too hard.* I feel you. I've been there, too. *Oof.* To be sure, there may be much that clamors for you to live in fear, fatigue, and scarcity. Your current reality may be that you feel bone-tired and desperately low on bandwidth, with no place to rest in sight. Life can seem heavy and hard when fear and anxiety about what hasn't yet happened, what you still don't have, and what is wrong preoccupy your mind. Consider for a moment what recent research in the field of neuroscience has shown us: whatever we focus on gets bigger. It grows.

This is where gratitude and looking for the good comes in. It's one of those simple, but not easy, practices. In the midst of life here and now—particularly in the hard, the painful, and the challenging—when you cultivate the habit of looking for the good, when you practice thankfulness in more bits of life, when you *really* remember it, you change.

The funk and difficulties may not be gone, but you are different and the world seems different. When your heart fills up and gets more jam-packed with *grateFULLness*, you begin to see the vastness, the plenty, and the abundance of gifts within your life and in the world around you. The mishaps and mistakes morph into building blocks of hope and the not-knowing doesn't stop you

> When your heart fills up and gets more jam-packed with *grateFULLness*, you begin to see the vastness, the plenty, and the abundance of gifts within your life and in the world around you.

from walking with your head held high and your eyes sparkling. The days shift to being fueled by your unstoppable purpose rather than by lack and overwhelm—from the time you rise until the time you fall into bed at night. Sounds pretty good, aye?

Let's take a moment to explore your day, one part at a time, weaving in PoPs—practices, perspectives, and *gratefulness*—to keep your battery charged and your focus where it will best serve you.

Morning. Imagine this. The alarm buzzes, chirping that it's time for your day to begin. The sun is streaming in your window, its rays beckoning you to awaken. Although still a bit tired and resistant to rising (it may be mighty cozy under those covers!), you stretch, take a deep breath, pull back the sheets, and find yourself more eager than groggy for the day to come. You softly smile at what lies ahead of you on this day.

What simple rituals or practices can you envision creating that would provide a morning experience filled with joy? How might they prevent you from being derailed by thoughts tinged with worry, overwhelm, or the unknown, allowing you to look right at them and respond with ease? What would cause you to increase the level of eagerness—a little or a lot—with which you greet your day? Is it sipping a cozy drink, sitting in a certain place, going for a walk or a run, reading, meditating, writing, or creating a bit more time for getting ready?

Midday. Is there a five-minute midday opportunity each day when you might consider the *good* that's happened in the morning, and pause, breathe, and go outside? On the warm days, might you take a walk, feeling the sun warming your skin or the cool breeze touching you? On days that are too chilly or too wet to head outside, could you sit at a window and look out at nature with a steaming cup of tea?

Evening. How might you end your day each night—is there anything you might shift that would fuel and sustain you with a bit more feel-good juju as you look back at your day and forward to the day ahead? Is it getting to bed earlier, sitting with your partner over a delicious evening drink, taking a bath, reading an inspirational book, or listening to a piece of music that swells your heart?

You need these rhythms and ways of *DOing* and *BEing* as surely as you need air to breathe.

PoP

3 Be Still (surrender)

Take this moment, whatever time of day it is,
wherever you find yourself, and just be.
This is not the time to do, think, plan, consider.
Breathe. Relax.
Stay here, for a few or many minutes.

ponder (go deeper)

Listen to "Perfect Timing (This Morning)" by Orba
Squara. Imagine some of the elements of your perfect
morning stretching into your day and evening. Write
about it or walk and *ponder* it.

How are your daily PoPs feeling and working? Are you
settling into a rhythm that feels good to you? If not, write
a bit about deepening your practice and commitment to
a daily PoP. Get detailed about it: time of day, length
of PoP, place, other elements—including a cozy drink,
books, journal.

What might be ways for you to take a pause midday
or end your day that will feel good, fuel you, and bring
renewed strength and vitality into your life? Try them. See
which ones you like most, and commit to regularly cultivating them in your life.

Do you feel the *low battery* warning go off regularly? What can you imagine implementing as portable charging stations for the road—to fuel you up during the day as needed? How do you *charge up* yourself for the daily rigors that are bound to occur? Are there practices you notice other people doing that would be fun to try when responding to stress in the moment or low energy during your day?

Keep in mind that a spontaneous, spur-of-the-moment PoP can be a powerful way to respond when life hits you with a stressful trigger. Taking some time to pause, ponder, and consider what you want to do to engage with the challenge from a place of wisdom, truth, voice, courage, and love can lead to intentional actions rather than knee-jerk reactions.

Would your heart and life be buoyed a bit by gratitude? Write about what would shift. Explore if there are any specific places or relationships in which you'd like to commit to being more *grateFULL*. If you have a moment, check out GoodGoodGood.co online. It is all about cultivating the good through celebrating and becoming accomplices in good work. Their print *Goodnewspaper* and online e-newsletter, the *Goodnewsletter,* are stunning examples of looking for the good. How about creating your own daily *Goodnewsletter* and writing one gratitude each day in a journal, on your bathroom mirror, or via a text to yourself?

3

Engage (commit)

A nudge. Commit to a pocket of time today to *be* in silence, when there is typically noise and conversation. Try it. Turn off the radio, your TV, maybe even play with having a meal in silence with those in your life ... explore what bubbles up. If you like it, do it again tomorrow.

Now, it's your turn. What or who are you beckoned to *commit to, connect with,* or *create*—whether in small or big ways?

Share something from this PoP with someone you trust.

BE BOLD. BE BRAVE. BE YOU.

2

[flickering]

shining with a wavering light. burning
irregularly or unsteadily.

when life is hard

If you are reading this
with a heart or body throbbing with pain,
I'm sending love to you, intending and praying
for you to feel seen, companioned, and supported.
The struggle need not be the end of your story.

Do you lament?
"I can't do this. I'm stuck."
"I can't imagine lighting UP the world."
"There is way too much that's broken in my own life."
If so, you're not alone.

There can be pain—great oceans of it—
in us, around us.
Allow what is broken in you or in the world
to capture your attention.
Pause and tend to these places.
You will find surprises and treasures here—
in these deep chasms lie gemstones.

Out of the darkest places,
the pain that cripples and blinds, right here,
there is love, hope, and healing.

Struggling

BEING HUMAN CAN BE HARD.

Bugger moments of heartbreak arise in and around you all the time.

Maybe life has been clipping along at a satisfactory—or spectac-ular—rate, but you are aware of pain in the life of someone you love or in the lives of those in far-off places. Or perhaps it's been a really tough week, month, and year for *you* … a too-long-stretch of hard days filled with confusion and overwhelm. The everyday human strains of health, finances, relationships, or work may have fallen heavy and hard in your lap.

A nudge: Don't run way. Stay here. The goodness to be discov-ered often lies among the hard, the dark, and the brutal. Although struggle need not have the last word in your story, there is a step you must take before getting to the joy, freedom, and healing.

You must acknowledge. You must see. You must look. At what has hurt. At what terrifies. At what is hard. In the world around you. In the lives of those you love. Within you.

Yes, you. Herein lies the root of your story. This story is your very own. There is a great gift in owning and embracing the whole of your story. However you see or feel about it, even if it seems ordi-nary, insufficient, meaningless, too broken, or not enough in some way, I invite you to look at it. Dare I nudge you further? *Wrap your arms around* the good, the bad, and the ugly that has happened to you or to those you love in days past or maybe even today.

> A nudge. Don't run way. Stay here. The goodness to be discovered often lies among the hard, the dark, and the brutal.

The same invitation is there for you as you encounter those around you. This is an important part of the *we* story—the bigger global human family of which you are an integral, important, and imperative part. Pay attention to what matters to you in the world around you, what captures your attention, and what pains you. There are vital clues here—uncomfortable as they may be—that will light up your path. What breaks or has broken your heart is a mighty piece of your why, what, who, and the clarification of your one-of-a-kind purpose on the planet.

Your experience of heartbreak can open you up more deeply to the Sacred and to your tribe. In my spiritual tradition, there is a text that invites us to talk with God in a never-stopping sort of way about anything and everything. When it comes to pain and struggle, there is a lot to talk about. It can flow all day long. Continually. Without ceasing.

In my life, the more I do it, the better life is. Whether I whisper or shout it, I share my dreams, hopes, burdens, and pain with God. In this way, each kicked-in-the-gut moment becomes a steady, unceasing, sacred stream of conversation. When my heart breaks at the pain in the world, I pound the gates of heaven asking for help, for forces greater than me to advocate and fight for the rights and dignity of people. There is another tenor to this pounding as well. I ask to be shown my part, my next steps of action and connection. When I do, I am often drawn to connect with and take action among my tribe of soul friends and my mighty human family.

In this way, *prayer propels* us to be connected, to keep it real, to act in the midst of our ever-unfolding stories. This concept that *prayer propels* came out of a text thread between my treasured circle of soul sisters. We have committed to keep it wholly real and to hold each other close in prayer when hope is flickering low. One friend recently reached out with this: "So if you would pray, the situation here is dark." That was it. Ten words. Just ten words opened up a steady flow of pings that pulsed with hope and kept her from spiraling into grieving isolation.

It was a moment of unstoppable conversation with God and with one another. It was a picture of contemplative *BEing* and active *DOing*. One of my favorite promises in my spiritual tradition says that when two or more people are *together* in prayer, Spirit is *right there*. For

> The wound is the place where the Light enters you.
> -Rumi

years, I have been curious about this invitation and promise, but I see it more clearly than ever now. It connects us. It keeps us committed to walk through life together. Whether called meditation, prayer, or something else, talking with the always-present Sacred in that never-stopping way is simple. And it changes everything.

Messaging

IT IS TOO LATE.
I DO NOT MATTER.
I HAVE NOTHING TO OFFER.
I DO NOT HAVE WHAT I NEED.
I AM ALONE-ALWAYS HAVE BEEN, ALWAYS WILL BE.
THERE IS NO GOOD THAT CAN COME FROM THIS SITUATION.
BECAUSE I DID THIS (OR DIDN'T DO THAT), THERE IS NO HOPE.

When unseen and unacknowledged, diminishing messages and thoughts can crush you. They wage war. They pervasively dishearten, leaving you listless and dreamless.

But when you know the ones to which you are most vulnerable, you can be on the lookout for them and you can to replace them with words that are expansive and true.

The power of the messages in this toxic self-talk is in their impact to lure you into believing that they will always be true and that hope is lost. When they are *tinged with truth*, they can loom even bigger. For instance, at times, you may indeed find yourself low on money, time, energy, or support. But, take heart. These small-minded messages are not ultimately true. Every last bit of your life, particularly the hard and hopeless bits, can be transformed into glittering gifts. Thus, *nothing* should cause you to hang your head with shame or embarrassment. *Nothing* should silence your voice. *Nothing* disqualifies you from continuing to hope, walk, and dream. *Nothing*. Not broken relationships, not seeming to have it all together, not being at rock bottom, not being wealthy or poor.

As you go about your day-to-day life, watch for the feelings of hopelessness that these messages often leave in their wake. When you have a decision to make or have a task to do, if you feel a lingering sense of discouragement, look for the feelings and motives behind these false messages and reach out for your tribe. Don't go it alone.

For many years, I have been deeply susceptible to living small and isolated by these untrue messages. As I see them more clearly and live more connected to my tribe, they fuel my thoughts and direct my decisions far less frequently.

A recent example is when I had a decision to make. Not a big one, but it evidenced a lifelong pattern of tumultuous uncertainty. Smack dab in the middle of two back-to-back conferences I wanted to attend was the first week of school for my two young kids. Internal thoughts started to clamor for my attention: *Don't even think about going. What kind of mom would miss the first day of school for her kids? Not a good one, that's for sure.* Before long, I was heading toward a spiral of confusion and worry.

> Every last bit of your life, particularly the hard and hopeless bits, can be transformed into glittering gifts.

Those pesky voices do that. They confuse us with their clamor. They silence us with their shame. They diminish us with their darts.

But not this time. This time, I really, *really* paused. I got quiet. I pondered. I listened. I took a walk. I wrote a bit about it in the pages of my journal. I prayed. In these moments, I saw the ways in which these diminishing messages had, unbeknownst to me, greatly influenced parts of my identity as a wife, mom, and in my work ... for quite some time. I was living too small in each of these treasured vocations.

Realizing I needed some outside perspective, I looped in a few trusted soul friends who understood my struggle and asked them what they saw that I might be missing. They opened my eyes to possibilities I hadn't yet seen. The clamor of voices grew quieter, the fog cleared bit by bit, and I saw my next step. I did head to the conference, but the real treasure was the path to this particular yes.

The process of discerning this *little* decision had a *big* internal impact. Old and persistently limiting messages connected to my identity lost their power. It was a catalyst for letting go of too-small notions related to my vocations of motherhood, marriage, and my work. Rooted in the simple, ordinary, and everydayness of life, this decision fostered more freedom and boldness than ever before within me.

Elevating the opinions or judgment of others is another way these thoughts can falsely guide and fuel, keeping you small and spinning in your thoughts and actions. Unchecked, these messages will morph into *people-pleasing*.

People-pleasing shackles. Constrains. Binds.

Know that what matters to you and how you envision showing up in life will not always be a crowd-pleaser. Be prepared for moments when what you dream to do will not make sense to everyone around you. Your way of being or doing things is unique to you, and not everyone will deem it significant. Do not wait for their affirmation and applause before you take a step or leap to live your purpose on the planet.

Keep crafting the story of your life, less influenced by these diminishing messages and the applause of others. You will live more free and less fettered than ever. Keep walking and leaping, with your head held high. Keep dreaming, with that gleam in your eye.

Striving

OVER THE YEARS, I HAVE READ BOOKS BY MANY AN EXPERT TO UNCOVER MORE OF MY PALPABLE LIFE'S PURPOSE. I HAVE ENROLLED IN COURSES, GONE ON RETREATS, AND LIVED IN COMMUNITY. I HAVE WORKED AT IT. I HAVE BECOME MORE ME.

And yet, I see that I often stressed and strove in my becoming. I have often tried hard ... so hard ... too hard.

There have been seasons when I didn't know how to relax while on the *jOURney*, particularly in the midst of the unknown. There have been times when I put so much energy into figuring out my work, my destiny, and my part in the world that the joy of everyday living has been eclipsed.

> You may feel it is all up to you, that there is not enough, that if you only did one more thing or tried just a bit harder, all would be well.

My father-in-law, Mike, passed away a few years ago. Oh, how I loved him. He was quite extraordinary. He worked diligently and was one of the most successful people I've known. The story of his discovery that he needed hearing aids is a lighthearted and simple reminder that sometimes it's not about trying harder.

One evening, he and my mom-in-law, Sue, were talking over dinner. As she shared about her day, he needed to ask her more than once to repeat herself, and the end result is the stuff of belly-laughing family legend. Understandably, after one too many times of being asked to repeat herself, she got frustrated. Throwing up her arms, she exasperatedly exclaimed, "Well, honey, just *try harder*!" Incredulously, he looked at her. In that moment, it struck him. No matter how hard he tried to hear her, he couldn't. He started laughing … hard. In the midst of the laughter, he told her that in that moment, he knew … he needed hearing aids.

Not only is trying harder not always the answer to our challenges, but it can make challenges—big ones—crop up out of beautiful beginnings. I learned this when I had my babies, Sophia and Micah, born just a few years apart.

> Not only is trying harder not always the answer to our challenges, but it can make challenges—big ones—crop up out of beautiful beginnings.

While pregnant with each, I poured over baby books, delving into what to expect, what to eat, how to do my part to birth healthy babies. When they were born, I basked in their smells, their sounds, and the pure joy of just holding them. In the midst of the caring and wonder of this extraordinary vocation of motherhood, I set my sights on being a great momma. Nothin' wrong with that at a glance, but little by little, I ratcheted my pledge higher and higher toward what became impossible standards of motherhood.

In the midst of the intensification, I lost a bit—and ultimately, a lot—of myself. As I did, I grew more and more isolated. I became more inclined to determine the success of my day based on what I did or didn't get done, the cleanliness of my home, myself, and my kids (never a good idea in the messy world of babies). I began to feel that I was not a good enough mom, wife, friend, or human being. I was flailing.

Thank goodness for my tribe. They woke me up, asked insightful questions, listened, and fanned the flames of passion and purpose that they knew were in me.

One such moment stands out. I was on a walk with my baby, Micah, and a treasured sister, Vicki. Near the end of our walk, she took my hand, drawing us to a stop. She gently and wisely spoke that though she knew I loved being a momma, it seemed I was not living *wholly me*. It seemed that large parts of me were clouded over and hidden. She wondered if I'd become encumbered and a bit disoriented in my day-to-day caretaking of my kids. She asked if I felt any of that to be true. I tearfully whispered a yes to her compassionate query.

Without seeing it for myself, I'd become burdened by striving too hard in one of my beloved and significant vocations: being a momma to my kiddos. As I deepened these new learnings through my PoPs and began working them into the day to day of my life, the flickering flame grew brighter.

The energy of striving and trying harder is exhausting and often does not lead to the places we are bound and determined to go. It may feel as if a light switch has flipped off and life becomes heavy and laborious.

There is a nuance, a subtlety to watch for here. Clues that the switch has gone off are when you feel that unrelenting energy of forcing and hard work ... a furrowed brow, grinding teeth, tight jaw, gut in pretzel knots, and sleepless nights. Here, you may feel it is all up to you, that there is not enough, that if you only did one more thing or tried just a bit harder, all would be well. This is an exhausting hamster wheel that never stops. There is no end to the striving, the measuring of your attempts, the visions for what more you might do in this crazy loop.

I'm curious, my friend—are there any of these places in your life? Although you may be doing work you love, would you benefit from tweaking the way in which you're doing it? As you reflect on this, slow down a bit, talk with your tribe, and explore how you might do things differently. You will, step by step, become a bit more free ... and a lot more you.

Starving

THERE WAS A DAY THAT MY HOPE DWINDLED TO A FLICKER, MY VOICE QUIETED TO A WHISPER, AND I ALMOST DIED.

The truth is, not many people know this part of my story. I've been reluctant to share it because I'm a little embarrassed. Almost two decades ago, I nearly starved myself to death in a land of plenty. I was lost and very, very alone. I doubted that I mattered.

Let me back up. I was twenty years old and living in Hong Kong, on a global learning adventure. The first day I arrived at the school, a typhoon stormed through the town. I sat in a room in the school—my new living quarters—as gale force winds howled and rain pelted the tin roof above us. Just outside, there was a brick wall, and I had what seemed to be a vision of what was to come, combined with what felt like a conversation with God.

If it sounds far-fetched, I get it. But it's true. I had a daydream, a vision, in which I was fully awake. As I looked at this brick wall, I saw clear as day, in my imagination, the following scene: the brick wall I was looking at was dismantled, brick by brick, to the very ground. I sensed that this brick wall was *me*—it was my *life*—and although I didn't understand it, I knew that this dismantling was going to happen to me. *Oof.*

Right then and there, in the midst of the storm, in that very moment of vision and daydream, I experienced the palpable and personal presence of God. I felt mighty and capable arms wrap around me. I felt eyes of Love gaze on me with great affection, twinkling with tenderness. I

> I was lost and very, very alone. I doubted that I mattered.

sensed deep within myself a divine message—a pep talk of sorts. As wild as it sounds, I heard an almost-audible voice in my heart say: "Some critical cracks have formed in the foundation of your life. The hard days of dismantling will make it possible for your life to be built with much more stability and security that can sustain a *breathtaking life* beyond your wildest dreams. In it all, I am with you and for you ... I will never leave your side."

But between the promise of the *breathtaking life* to come and my current reality was a season I would barely survive. I had chosen the school in Hong Kong intentionally; it offered me an opportunity to be immersed in a dynamic cross-cultural environment. It was the stuff of my dreams. Perhaps because I was the only American, and no doubt, due to other factors I don't fully understand, it was far from the experience I had expected. I felt repeatedly misunderstood and widely disliked. I felt a fundamental lack of belonging. As the days passed, my sense of self was shaken up and shattered. I fell hard and deep into depression, floundering and broken, with no idea of what to do. It was rough and I was dangerously solo in my pain.

> But, I wasn't really alone. Not then, not ever. Right then and there, God was with me, whispering encouragement to not give up, shoring up my broken spirit.

An eating disorder took hold in the dark days of struggle. Slowly and imperceptibly to me, diet and exercise began to drop my weight to dangerously low places. At that time, my vision of my purpose on the planet was foggy. I was shackled in my self-imposed cell by the choices I'd made and by internalized too-small thoughts. I was in a dark moment of the soul and body. My trusted tribe was far away, unaware of my downward spiral into addiction. I had never felt so alone.

But, I wasn't really alone. Not then, not ever. Right then and there, God was with me, whispering encouragement to not give up, shoring up my broken spirit. Those whispers kept me alive and helped me take the first steps away from death.

I left the school early and returned home to the United States in a deeply troubled state. The vision I'd had back in Hong Kong of stability and a life beyond my wildest dreams was dormant and invisible. I was utterly undone and wrecked. I found myself smack dab at rock bottom, in a deep pit of brokenness.

My days after I returned home were dark and sad ones. There was little room for anything in my life beyond my oppressive and obsessive calorie-counting and frenetic exercise. I slept for much of the day. My energy waned. Even then, there was a flicker—albeit a teeny-tiny one—of hope, a deep compelling commitment to not give up. To choose life.

As is often the case, the spark that I needed to wake up and to choose life did not occur in isolation. It came from another in my tribe. More specifically, it came from my mom as she was going about her day-to-day of taking care of her family—caring for and doing battle for her floundering, flickering daughter. One afternoon, she came to collect and fold what she thought was a crumpled blanket on the sofa and found me sleeping under it, my body so small that she couldn't see me underneath.

Her surprised gasp woke me up. In that moment, *I woke up.* I was struck by an overpowering knowing: *If I don't make some drastic changes, I won't make it much longer.* I needed help, and I knew it.

My family and I found a counselor who specialized in caring for those with eating disorders, and I joined a therapy group of women. We gathered once a week, each one of us so very small in body and imagination, but not yet ready to give up living … not just yet. In this keepin'-it-real, coffee, and tea-sipping circle, I heard a story that planted the seed that grew into an epiphany. One woman, twice my age, told of her decades-long battle with anorexia. She spoke of her pain, of her longing for more vitality, of her itty-bitty dreams and broken relationships. She was not happy. It was not a path of exciting and compelling purpose; it was brittle and little. It gave me a picture of my life in twenty years if I continued to walk in that direction. I knew with all my heart and being that I did not want her story to be my story. But, without a change, this *would* be me in twenty years.

After this moment of epiphany, things moved astonishingly fast. A crystal-clear plan came to mind. It was simple. From my healthy vantage point now, it is terribly obvious, but in the state of my addiction at the time, it was simply miraculous. This terribly obvious and simply miraculous plan was this: for thirty days, I would listen and respond to my body's intrinsic appetite. I would eat when I was hungry. I would trust my body's capacity to move me towards a more healthy weight. It was a simple, but not necessarily an easy, path. It was my thirty-day leap toward life.

I gained thirty pounds in thirty days—to the pound, to be exact, of what my therapists said was needed. For those of you who do not know about the world of eating disorders, this is most extraordinary. This sort of thinking and behavior rarely happens out of the blue or at this rate for someone in the grips of anorexia, as I was. It was most unusual and phenomenal. And it set me back on the path towards a *breathtaking life beyond my wildest dreams*.

I have been curious about the weeds in my youth that began to choke out the many other good, beautiful, and true parts, resulting in this rock-bottom season of darkness. Flipping back the pages in my story, I do remember my first moment of shameful body awareness. I was twelve. I was in the car, heading home from a softball game. Suddenly, my attention was riveted by my legs jiggling in my white, skin-tight softball uniform. *My legs are fat*, I thought as we drove down the road. It was the first time I remember having such a thought, and not knowing what to do with it, I did nothing. As weeds are wont to do when given space, this idea grew and flourished, watered by my hang-ups and the everyday challenges of growing up.

The best I can tell from this vantage point, twenty-five years later, is that the roots of my eating disorder were strengthened by a few factors. They developed in unchecked, unrelenting, and untrue messages. They took over even more as I habitually looked for affirmation from others and tried harder. They were rooted in my flawed belief that my value and worth were connected to and elevated by my performance and success.

At the heights of my brokenness, I developed the habit of measuring the centimeters of circumference around my leg. My measuring point was a freckle, a few inches above my knee. I would take a measuring tape, starting at the freckle, and wrap it around my thigh. I was hoping to decrease the measurement bit by bit. *That was crazy.* Wrapping a measuring tape around my thigh and evaluating myself, down to the tiniest of measurements: a centimeter? *Ridiculous.* Yet, I continued to do it.

Decades ago, I stopped that absurd (and rather embarrassing-to-share) pattern of measuring. However, there are other more subtle patterns that I need to keep an eye out for today, especially when it comes to my thoughts. Noxious and invasive thoughts matter, no matter how benign they may seem. If left unchecked and given space, they can cause great damage and devastation even in my life today. For example, my need to try harder (yes, still working at that one), and

> Weak is the New Strong.
> Because
> there's
> nothing
> left
> to
> prove.
> God isn't playing the game
> so why would we?
> And grasping clinging
> earning comparing ranking
> is exhausting.
> –Rob Bell

prove my value can derail me. Especially when I am overly tired or feeling weak, I am vulnerable to appraising my attempts in other arenas, too, whether personal, professional, or relational. At those times of feeling *less than*, I come up short. Yet, deep down, I know I need not measure or prove one more thing. You need not measure or prove one more thing either. And yes ... that is good news.

How I hope that you have never experienced this kind of dangerous addiction and rock-bottom doubt, loneliness, and fear. But, perhaps my story sounds strikingly familiar to yours. Perhaps you have found your story in bits of mine. Whether the connection is from years past or where you are right now, shine a light, speak your truth, and get some support for what you need right here and now. Fan and make brighter the flame of your life ... of your story. When you do, the darkness of the past, and even current challenges, are less scary and less palpable. There is hope, my friend, in speaking what is true, in shining the light on these dark places, and in claiming that this does not need to be the way things always will be in your story.

Wounding

WHEN I WAS AT THE PEAK OF MY EATING DISORDER, MY MIND, BODY, AND SOUL WERE SO DIS-EASED THAT THERE WAS LITTLE SOLACE IN TALKING TO OR BEING WITH OTHERS.

I remember those days, and they were gut-wrenching. Yet, in those days, more than ever, I needed people around me who lived with hope, a sense of vibrancy in their life, and who were dreaming big dreams. I needed their love and presence in my day-to-day life—it was one of the very things that kept me alive.

Are you walking wounded because of choices you've made that have encumbered or shackled you with addiction? If you stay alone in the pain, the regret, the shame, and the chaos of confusion, these wounds can leave you limping, hemorrhaging, and in the emergency room of life for many, many years—sometimes for an entire lifetime. There is another way. It need not be one of prolonged isolation, ache, or gripping pain.

Take heart, dear friend. There are times when words fail to communicate our deep places of hurt. If this moment finds you gripped by great pain and walking wounded, this is a time when I imagine us sitting together in my living room by the fire with a cup of steaming tea or slowly strolling together in that *bistari* way.

I hope this moment is imbued with some magic and that it touches you in a mysterious way. May whatever you most need slip into a crack in the doorway to your heart and fill you today. May you feel less alone. May you feel a flicker of hope, of a future, of love—perhaps a sense of anticipation for the days to come that you've not felt for a long time.

> When the words stop
> And you can endure
> the silence
> That reveals your heart's
> pain
> Of emptiness
> Or that great
> wrenching-sweet longing.
> That is the time
> to try and listen
> To what the Beloved's eyes
> most want to say.
> -Hafiz

The word, *BEloved*, is one to sit with here and now. Soulfully consider if there is something to be discovered in living more loved than ever before. Might it hold solace for your soul, your body, your heart? If you are in a place of health and strength, might you enter into this next PoP with an intention to think about, send some good juju, or pray for someone you know who is currently in a place of pain and darkness?

▶4 Be Still (surrender)

Be here.
Breathe.
Relax.
Let go.
BEloved.

ponder (go deeper)

Listen to the song, "You Are Loved," sung by Stars Go Dim. You *are* loved. You are glittering in value and worth. Write the words or feelings that pique your attention.

This time to be still is a keenly important one, dear one. Particularly if there is a wound you carry. If so, linger here a bit longer. What are you thinking, feeling, hoping, and longing for? Maybe you don't feel critically wounded, but you are hurt. How do you allow yourself to be human, to feel sad or angry, when you have been injured? Are there ways you pretend or deny that woundedness, feigning that you're good when you're really not? *Be real. Be you.*

Take whatever feels chaotic, painful, or broken in you. Really think about it. Imagine it. What does it look, sound, and feel like? Imagine Spirit hovering over it like a bird. What happens? Stay here for a moment. Even if nothing happens right now, in your way with your voice, ask for what you really want and need. Ask for an experience of peace and hope to be yours, right here and now. Be expectant. Be watchful. This can be a lifeline. Spirit is with you, has never left you, loves you with a big love, and can buoy and *enCOURAGE* you throughout each and every season of life.

Are there sacred texts in your life that speak to a promise that gives you hope in the pain? In my spiritual tradition, one of my favorite claims is that God promises to work astonishing good out of unspeakable pain. Even the injustice, the unfair, the abuse, the mistreatment. All of it. Does this give you solace? Is it something for you to walk with, meditate on, and contemplate? Does it give you a flicker of hope?

Engage (commit)

A nudge. Light a candle for a person who is wounded and capturing your heart's attention, whether near or far. *This person may be you.* Allow the flicker of the flame to be an act of prayer or meditation. Imagine the light of this candle warming the wounded one and kindling the flickering flame of hope.

Now, it's your turn. What or who are you beckoned to *commit to, connect with,* or *create*—whether in small or big ways?

Share something from this PoP with someone you trust.

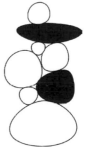

BE BOLD. BE BRAVE. BE YOU.

healing & hurting

Companioning one another
through the small and big hazards that come with life
is one of our great invitations and callings.
We can heal and we can hurt one another
as we go about our day-to-day living.

Our mighty human family can and has perpetuated
grave injustices upon its own members.
And yet, we can be the very hands and feet
that bring healing and hope to one another.

I invite you to simply, yet radically,
reorient your vision and capacity for your part
in the world's great beauty, complexity, and struggles.
In this colossal collective,
you will find the courage and commitment
to excavate and cultivate the gold, the good,
and the glimmering hope
in the midst of the dark.

Choosing

MY DAUGHTER, SOPHIA, RECENTLY TOOK PART IN A BLINDFOLDED TRUST WALK ON A COMMUNITY-BUILDING HIKE WITH HER CLASSMATES.

Verbal cues were to be given by a partner when it was time to turn, slow, or step over an obstacle. Maybe he didn't see what was coming or he was distracted, but for whatever reason, her guide gave no cue at a critical moment.

Sophia slammed headfirst into a pole. *Whoof! Clunk!* A scar still marks the spot on her forehead.

My girl is not the only one to be let down by someone in whom trust has been placed. No doubt, you can recall an occasion or two when you have been less-than-supported by people in your life. I sure do. You may still be feeling the sting of such an experience or carry a scar, whether outwardly visible or not. Those poles we walk into tend to leave some kind of mark.

As you build your tribe, this is a key invitation to be discerning about those you choose for your inner circle of trusted soul friends. Do not put on a blindfold and be led on your journey by just anyone. Any community or tribe is made up of humans, and humans always have flaws and imperfections that can cause injury in either inadvertent or intentional ways. Herein lies a dynamic invitation to live connected and engaged with others in your mighty collective *and* to do so wisely. You need others—chosen *care-FULLY*—to walk with you.

Comparing

THE PRISMATIC BEAUTY OF THIS MIGHTY HUMAN FAMILY IS THAT EACH ONE OF US HAS DISTINCTIVE GIFTS AND INDIVIDUAL WAYS TO OFFER THEM TO THE WORLD.

We cannot wholeheartedly participate in this diverse tribe if we get caught in the hook of comparing our unique strengths and purposes with one another. Some of us are wildly exuberant extroverts, others steadfast introverts.

Some of us may be committed to tend to those closest to us, while others of us feel drawn to support those who live far away. Some of us may have work to do that is visibly significant, while others' work may be quieter in its impact. Our world is full of amazing people doing unbelievably remarkable things that are making a significant difference. We need it all. No one way is better than another.

I speak to this challenge of comparing, because I know it well. At times in my life, I have compared myself to the astounding others around me, which has clouded and stunted my vision. For example, at times, I've compared myself to my mom and mother-in-law, who are two of the most extraordinary caretakers and homemakers on the planet. The moment you walk through the doors of their homes, there is beauty—from the full pantry and 'fridge, to the cleanliness of their homes, each having created households of vibrant, jaw-dropping hospitality. At times, I've found myself lacking when it comes to the spotlessness of my home or in the making of home-cooked family dinners.

When I am tired, isolated, in a funk, feeling a bit "off," or feeling too open to those diminishing messages, I am susceptible and vulnerable to sliding into shriveling comparisons. At those times, I measure and assess myself on the *DOing* scale, again finding myself lacking. In response, I hustle, strive, and try too hard.

Comparing sets up all of us for living small, flickering lives. It's an epic and mighty waste of time. We are all in such different places in this journey. Wherever you find yourself, in this moment, right now, I offer a nudge: relax a bit, let go, and pay attention to your own story and your personal longings without determining them better or worse than another's. You may be ready to make small shifts by weaving new ways of feel-good inspired action into your daily life. Or you may have already made, or are about to make, gigantic shifts related to your career, focus, and unstoppable purpose on the planet. Wherever you are is perfect. Choose to live in ways that are unique to you.

> Wherever you find yourself, in this moment, right, I offer a nudge: relax a bit, let go, and pay attention to your own story and your personal longings without determining them better or worse than another's.

Witnessing

IT TAKES COURAGE-LOTS OF IT-TO KEEP IT REAL AND TO ALLOW PEOPLE INTO OUR LESS-THAN-PERFECT MOMENTS.

The imperfections, challenges, and conundrums in *EVERYday* life offer a plethora of opportunities to learn, to expand, and to deepen our connections with those in our tribe.

It's not always easy. It's often uncomfortable and vulnerable to grow in the company of others. I call this witnessing.

Witnessing is a dynamic commitment to find simple and powerful ways to companion people. This, too, is rooted in the everyday of life. It'll keep you on your toes, with your eyes and heart wide open. Sometimes it means that you champion and celebrate what you see in those around you. At other times, it means you will sit with and say nothing to one who is struggling … just being with another person who is in pain can be a most extraordinary act. They don't need to be alone or hide in a challenging moment. Sometimes it means speaking and calling attention to what a person may not see as a blind spot or a historical pattern that is eclipsing freedom and joy in their life.

One such event occurred when I was *almost derailed by a floating tablecloth*. This story took place many years ago. I was in high school, working as part of the dining staff at a youth summer camp. While cleaning up, I shook out a tablecloth over the banister. Unbeknownst to me, hidden inside was a second tablecloth, along with napkins and a cling-clang bunch of forks, knives, and spoons. The spot where I stood, shaking out the tablecloth, was perched high above a bay. As if in slow motion, the tablecloth and its contents drifted down to the water, capturing the attention of the campers teeming by the pool below. They howled with laughter, pointing at the flatware as it went *plunk, plunk, plunk,* followed by the tablecloth as it glided gracefully into the water.

That's it. That's all that happened. Seems like no biggie, right? So, where in the world is the story of *derailment*? Well, to have a bunch of my peers witness a foolish mistake, albeit a small one, was huge and difficult to weather at that stage in my life. I was mortified and oh, so embarrassed.

I ran and looked for a place to hide, finding the only private place where I knew to go—the kitchen storage room. It was dark, and I could be invisible there. In hidden seclusion, I cried. *Hard.* I hadn't been much of a crier as a kid, but I made up for a bunch of no-crying days that afternoon. I was a blubbering mess.

One of the treasured elders of my teenage years, Stu, had been with the kids poolside and witnessed what had happened. He knew me well. He understood my propensity to take myself way too seriously and to be a bit tough on myself, no matter how big or small the mishap. He had a hunch I would be struggling and figured I would be in need of a friend. Stu looked until he found me in the storeroom.

> It's not always easy. It's often uncomfortable and vulnerable to grow in the company of others. I call this witnessing.

He sat down next to me and asked what was going on. He mostly listened and shared a few wise words. Stu has a gift of levity, so in no time, we were laughing as we sat together. He pulled me up off the floor and suggested we head outside. We walked and talked about the ways in which I was burdened and shackled by the shame of my imperfections and my quest to be flawless.

> Practicing courage, compassion, and connection in our daily lives is how we cultivate worthiness. The key word is practice. Mary Daly, a theologian, writes, "Courage is like—it's a habitus, a habit, a virtue: You get it by courageous acts. It's like you learn to swim by swimming. You learn courage by couraging."
> -Brené Brown, *The Gifts of Imperfection*

As we walked and talked, this minuscule mistake took on a different texture. It became more communal than solitary. More loving than shaming. More liberating than derailing. *Ahh.*

Of course, even alone, I would have emerged from that storage room at some point. But, with Stu's help, it was a fundamentally different experience, one with more levity and learning than would have occurred if I'd tried to navigate my struggle solo.

Witnessing is one of our great callings as a collective, as a tribe. Stick with it, my friend. There is gold here, in this sweet company. You will be more free. *Free to be bold. Free to be brave. Free to be you.* And you will usher in the same freedom, boldness, and bravery in those around you.

Lamenting

I THINK ABOUT MY DEAR FRIEND, FATOUMA. FATOUMA'S HEART CRACKED IN TWO WHEN HER SON PASSED AWAY LAST YEAR. HER WAILS OF LAMENT WILL REMAIN IN MY HEART AND EARS FOREVER.

According to her Islamic faith tradition, for forty days of *du'ua*, of prayer and mourning, her tribe of sisters and brothers gathered and encircled her. She did not mourn or pray alone. We lit candles, brought food, prayed, sang, and cried, together.

One day, she said to us, "I am a very strong woman, but without you and Allah, peace be upon Him, I wouldn't have made it. There is no doubt in my mind; I wouldn't have made it through this alone. I am African, Muslim, woman, grandma, sister, mother, wife, aunt, friend. Allah, peace be upon Him, gave me everything. He has given me the world as my family. He gave me you."

> When it comes to the big stuff, the really hard days, we are not meant to find solutions or care for ourselves alone.

Her sacred text, the Quran, speaks to this: "And as for the believing men and the believing women, they are guardians of each other; they enjoin good and forbid evil and keep up prayer."

When it comes to the big stuff, the really hard days, we are not meant to find solutions or care for ourselves alone. The greater the struggle, the greater the grief, the more we need each other. Sometimes, our lives depend on it.

pop

5 *Be Still (surrender)*

Sit down.
Lean back, rest your head.
Prop up your feet.
Three breaths, slow inhales, deep exhales.
Stay here ... for as long as you can, need, want.

ponder (go deeper)

Listen to the song, "All Through the Night," sung by Sleeping at Last. Write about and explore in your own way what strikes you in this song-poem of being with one another in the midst of the dark nights. If you feel alone in your struggle, consider how this might be a dream or a prayer for support, for companions in the midst of the hard.

Has there been a time when you were the recipient of this tender loving care while in the depths of despair? Was it easy or difficult to accept? Think on or write about the details—the feelings, the place, the response in you to it all.

Has there been a time of great sorrow in your life when you felt alone? Perhaps you didn't feel comfortable reaching out to others for the support you needed. What made it difficult for you to ask for support? If that time is now, sit with this nudge: Is there one person you can call, text, or email today? Right here, is there one person with whom you can share your raw and real story?

Engage (commit)

A nudge. Set a date to gather some folks to explore and dream together how you might extend some care to someone or a community in need of support.

Now, it's your turn. What or who are you beckoned to *commit to, connect with,* or *create*—whether in small or big ways?

Share something from this PoP with someone you trust.

BE BOLD. BE BRAVE. BE YOU.

look for & find

To those who feel vulnerable, invisible, lost, silenced,
hungry, hopeless, or hurting—
we hear and see you.

We are coming and are gathering many more,
each claiming and using
our unique purpose on the planet
to be with you, to enCOURAGE,
listen to, collaborate,
and learn from you.

We pledge to do whatever we can.
We do not have the answers,
but we are committed to a life with you
in which we cultivate hope and a future.
You are not alone.
You are not invisible.
Crying may remain for a night, but joy is coming.

YOU DO NOT NEED TO DIG DEEP TO FIND PAIN IN OUR WORLD.

Most likely, steady streams of ticker tape lines scroll across the bottom of your TV screen and your cell phone chimes with news updates of the horrifying and the unimaginable.

What to do? You know that these challenges are mighty, and you may feel at a loss for what you can possibly do to make a difference.

You may be nudged to move toward what beckons—and maybe what breaks—your heart. This takes courage. You've got this, because you guessed it—you're not alone.

In the stories to come, witness the courage and commitment of those who chose to wade into the deep of the pain in our world. Despite the crush and the deep pain, the arc of each of these stories is aglow with inspiration, hope, and great big love.

May you find a bit more of what matters to you in the stories that follow.

Called to Craters

IT WAS 1992, DURING THE SIEGE OF SARAJEVO. IN NEARLY FOUR YEARS, TEN THOUSAND PEOPLE WERE KILLED IN THE CITY OF SARAJEVO, THE CAPITAL OF BOSNIA AND HERZEGOVINA.

One day, in the midst of the conflict, cellist Vedran Smailović received word that twenty-two fellow citizens had been bombed. They died waiting in line for bread.

Tragic. Terrifying. Unjust. Unfair.

It would be understandable if he went home and stayed there, behind locked doors, as long as he could. The world outside was on fire, terror-stricken, and there was little hope in sight. But that is not what he did. No, Vedran did something extraordinary that is still being talked about today, more than two decades later. He went home, packed up his cello, and stepped out his door. He was on a mission. With cello in hand, he walked to where the bomb had fallen, planted himself in the crater left by the bomb in the midst of the rubble, and began to play. He called this act a *protest in the darkness,* and he returned daily, for twenty-two days, in memoriam of each person who had died.

As the killing continued, so did his cello-protest in the darkness. Day in and day out, the notes of his cello intermingled with the ricochet of sniper fire around him. Eventually called "The Cellist of Sarajevo," he traveled to funerals and places of devastation until the seemingly interminable killing ended in 1996. What he did took courage. It was dangerous.

Vedran said in the *New York Times* article of June 8, 1992, "I am nothing special, I am a musician, I am part of the town. Like everyone else, I do what I can." The cello was a simple, *EVERYday*, ordinary object for Vedran. In the face of unimagina-

> In the face of unimaginable and continuous death and destruction, he picked up his tool, gave what he could, and tended to what was right in front of him.

ble and continuous death and destruction, he picked up his tool, gave what he could, and tended to what was right in front of him.

You also have a one-of-a-kind gift and purpose. You might even think of it as a unique song you sing or a tool you wield as you move through your days. Whatever it might be, you have something that will bring beauty, companionship, or meaning into the bomb craters and war zones of the lives of those around you.

Do you know what your "cello tool" is or can you hear your unique song yet? Have you not sung a word or a note yet, or have you been chanting it your whole life quietly or at the top of your lungs? Listen for the melody.

Pause. Listen. Wait. Look. Pay attention. The melody will come.

Play it. Sing it. Live it. When you do, you will wake up, come alive, and live ablaze.

Oh, the epic beauty that is generated when you live, singing your one-of-a-kind song. This *is* your purpose on the planet—right here and now. Your music will invite others to sing their songs too. Harmonies will happen. This is the astonishing artistry, a thing of beauty that births harmonious collaboration in our *jOURney together*.

Purpose in Pain

CLUES TO YOUR PURPOSE ON THE PLANET MAY BE SITTING RIGHT NEXT TO YOUR PAIN.

Christina Noble's life depicts just that. Breathtaking in resilience, her life of _comPASSIONate_ commitment has made life better for nearly a million children far away from the country of her birth.

Her life hasn't been easy. No, far from it. Before her story today of extraordinary impact, she navigated many years of excessive struggle. It was brutal and her heart was broken. More than once.

Born in Ireland in 1944, her mother died when she was ten, her father was held in the grip of alcoholism, and the family descended deeply into poverty. Christina and her siblings picked through garbage dumps for their food. As is too often the case in the world, violence shadowed her vulnerability, and she was raped as a teenager. Once married, her husband physically and emotionally abused her.

Gut-wrenching. Unfair. Unjust.

Though it seemed this was her devastating lot in life and there was nothing she could do to change it, mercifully, this was not the end of her story. She tenaciously persevered, step by challenging step.

As a teenager, in the midst of days of tremendous trials, she had a dream one night of a distant land, Vietnam. She knew next to nothing about the country. So, although curious about its message,

Christina tucked this dream into her heart, not to be explored again for many years.

Twenty years later, she bought a one-way plane ticket to Vietnam, fueled by a hunch and a hope that embedded in that teenage dream was a clue to her destiny. The very day she landed, her heart was immediately captured by the children on the street.

Her birth country of Ireland and Vietnam were far away from each other, with very different cultures. But she quickly discovered that the vulnerable poor children in both places were not so dissimilar. Remembering her own impoverished childhood, she understood their hunger as she saw them picking through garbage and knew their susceptibility to those who could exploit their vulnerability as they wandered the streets.

> Her dreams, destiny, and joy were nestled right alongside her personal pain and struggle. (As are yours.)

A fire was lit in Christina that has fueled a movement of jaw-dropping support of nearly one million vulnerable children. The Christina Noble Children's Foundation (cnct.org) provides access to education, healthcare, safe living environments, and a future illuminated by hope. Her work has expanded beyond Vietnam and today includes Mongolia.

To be sure, looking at Christina's story from a big picture vantage point, it appears epic in its impact and scope. Yet, the grand story began with small and simple steps. Despite great personal struggles, she kept walking. She didn't run away from her heartache. She dared to remember and trust that the dream she'd had as a teenager held a clue for her destiny. She waded into the deep to get close to the street children of Vietnam. And there, right there, she found the joy of a life of oceanic purpose and love.

Her dreams, destiny, and joy were nestled right alongside her personal pain and struggle. (As are yours.)

New Stories

WHEN YOU OFFER YOUR GIFTS—YOURSELF—TO THE WORLD, BREATHTAKING AND ASTONISHING THINGS HAPPEN.

The extraordinary powers of restoration and transformation out of seemingly dead-end stories often emerge as we become kindling companions and fuel for one another on the road. This is one of the most essential parts of life's adventure.

That's exactly what happened when an unlikely collaboration was forged between a tribe of surfers and veterans. *Resurface* is a fantastic film that tells the story of their inspiring partnership in response to a very real and serious need (resurfacethemovie.com).

The film states that in the U.S., twenty-two veterans kill themselves every twenty-four hours (and those are *only* the reported ones). In *Resurface*, the veterans speak of gut-wrenching struggles, of bodies being damaged by bombs and shrapnel, of spirits being crushed, and of tremendous guilt, pain, and hopelessness, without dreams for the future. In this film, we see how a community of surfers *waded into the deep* of this pain and committed to companion these men and women. In and out of the ocean, with Operation Surf, we see the lives of veterans ignited and renewed. The film portrays how the waves and this community collective have begun to wash away despondency and isolation. Seeds have been planted for a renewed vision for a *good life*.

One of the remarkable veterans, Bobby Lane, shares about his life-altering experience that sparked something brand new in him. "The plan was that I was gonna go surfing [something he'd wanted to do since he was a child], go home, make sure everything's in order and then I was gonna get my gun and I was gonna commit suicide. Operation Surf had a slot open ... so I could go surfing. I said, 'Well that's it. I'd feel like I had achieved everything that I wanted to achieve in life and I'd be okay with dying.'

"When I caught that wave, it felt like a part of me died. The body that was going through life hurting and in so much pain and guilt, that guy died out there that day. And I could feel ... the ocean's heartbeat, as if it was this living, breathing thing. It wasn't death and destruction, trauma and hell."

Right before our eyes, we witness a metamorphosis in this once suicidal veteran. "Surfing not only changed my life, but it saved my life." Bobby's epiphany ripples further. He continues, "It's kind of like I was given a second chance. If I'm going to go out, I'm going to go out the right way. Right now, I'm on a mission to live." He decided that if something like surfing could bring peace to his life, then he'd live on and try to help as many veterans as possible. Today, Bobby is doing just that, as he passionately serves veterans who are struggling mentally and physically. This fierce clarity and focus grew out of his very own rock-bottom days. Who better to listen to, speak to, and encourage these veterans than one who is kindred, who knows, and who has lived in the grips of dead-end darkness?

> Out of heartbreak, your roots will grow, strengthened by love, to cultivate healing in yourself and others.

Van Curaza is founder of Operation Surf. He speaks in the film about an epiphany of his own. "It started because all I wanted to do was take a group of veterans surfing. Ever since I started Operation Surf, it really came clear to me about what my purpose was. Working with these warriors in transition … it's important to me."

Bobby and Van found purpose and buoyant new stories, together. In the surfing and service. In the giving and receiving. In the purpose and pain.

Do you see it, hear it, feel it? These individuals offered what they had, from where they were, in the ways they could. This way of life is one of pulsing purpose and plentiful new beginnings.

This is part of our calling as a tribe: to see and invoke these new beginnings in one another, to foster this mighty *reset that restores*. There are times when it's a matter of life and death. It was for these veterans.

It's not only these brave veterans who need this restoring reset, though. There are times, seasons, and days when each one of us needs a new story, with changed habits, memories, and patterns of thought and action.

Be courageously honest about where you are and what pain exists in your life. It has the potential to illuminate your next steps and leaps. Bit by bit, your gaze and your path will become clearer, sharper, and more powerful than ever. Out of heartbreak, your roots will grow, strengthened by love, to cultivate healing in yourself and others.

Dignity from Dust

SHE IS HANDED A BLACK ROUND THING. HER HEART IS BEATING FAST BECAUSE SHE KNOWS WHAT THIS IS. A BOMB. HER NAME IS HANNAH.

She is eight years old, and she has no choice but to carry it. The year is 2003, and the Maoist rebels have been hiding out in her village in Nepal.

It's the ideal location, as not many care about her people, called the *Badi* (pronounced "body"). They have been legally categorized, since 1854, as *Pani Na Chalne* ("Impure and Untouchable") in Nepal's legal code. They are a despised people—the lowest ranked untouchable caste in western Nepal, called by many the "untouchables among the untouchables" and the "dust of Nepal." The Maoists figure they are safely invisible living among these *untouchables*, this *dust*.

"Careful," he tells her. "One wrong move and you'll blow up. You'll be dead."

Hannah knows this story well. She has been told what to do her whole life. As have her sisters, mother, and grandmothers. They are Badi women. They know what they cannot do: walk, eat, or drink with people of higher cultural standing and caste. No one wants to be near them, to touch them, to walk on the same village path as them ... until it comes to sex. When sex is desired, these *untouchable* Badi women become very *touchable*.

> The same girl who trudged through the jungle, with hands trembling as the bomb lay nestled in her fingers, living each day perpetually at risk of being sexually exploited, is leading a movement of her own people that is changing the future of many.

It hasn't always been such a struggle. The *Badi* haven't always been disdained and sexually objectified. Her people were esteemed artists in the courts of the kings of Nepal. Hannah's mother danced for the king. Their very name, Badi, means "musical people." But, over time, this gift was slowly perverted; so much so that Badi women have become lucrative objects sought after for sex trafficking and are taken to brothels throughout Asia, where they live enslaved for many years. Most are never permitted to leave. Some girls are kept in their villages in Nepal, where men crawl through their windows, asserting their right to have sex with them. "No" has not been a permissible answer.

Despite the prevailing messages that she was worthless and powerless to participate in community life outside of her own low caste, a longing for a different way compelled Hannah since she was a little girl. She was voracious in her hunger for an education from the start, but parents from other tribes didn't want their children in the same room with an untouchable girl, a Badi. Undeterred, she walked five miles to school, hiding quietly under an open window and craning her neck to try and catch the teacher's instruction. When discovered, she was forced to leave the school grounds, only to return the next day to try again. She persisted and kept returning to that window.

Even when she was being formed, still in her momma's stomach, Hannah's fate as a female Badi seemed to be locked in place — as a pleasurable sexual object and an exceedingly lucrative commodity. Submission to the power of men and of others in higher castes has been the only way for women in this people group. That is, until recently.

The same girl who trudged through the jungle, with hands trembling as the bomb lay nestled in her fingers, living each day perpetually at risk of being sexually exploited, is leading a movement of her own people that is changing the future of many. Hannah now travels the globe, speaking about her life and opening people's hearts to the realities of injustice in the world. She invites listeners to wake up and join the fight for freedom for all.

Hannah is a fierce warrior of love and justice, and she is just getting started. She's launching into her next big dream and will be the first Badi woman in history to attend university.

Because of Hannah and her community's collective vision and activism, a growing number of Badi women are being rescued from brothels, and many others have been spared from the horrors of sex trafficking for the first time in generations. Many Badi girls and boys are going to school, takings steps and leaps towards futures full-to-the-brim with purpose and possibility. They have more freedom than ever before and are rising from the ashes. A new story is being kindled, and the glow of hope is brighter than ever.

I was with Hannah in her village in the far west of Nepal when her big sister, Alisha, returned home for the first time after her rescue from a brothel in India, where she had lived as a sex slave for twenty-one years. I have a vivid memory of Alisha leaning on the doorframe of her childhood home, eyes sparkling, mouth slightly turned up to a gentle smile, hand softly resting on her momma's shoulder, and her toes tapping to the beat of her father's drum and song. As Alisha watches, Hannah whirls her powerful and beautiful dance, bare feet beating the dirt floor of her family's porch.

Hannah is whirling and smiling, despite having experienced and seen more unspeakable disregard for human dignity and security than most of us can imagine, let alone understand. Her smile lights up a room with joy, she speaks with deep reservoirs of hope, and carries herself with a bold and formidable spirit. Her love is not weak sauce, airy-fairy. It propels her to go into places of danger and of desperation, returning to the very brothel that enslaved her sister in order to rescue more girls and women. Her faith is alive and sustains her vision. It's the real deal, having seen her through many moments of brutality and hopelessness.

> Hope is being able to see that there is light despite all the darkness.
> -Desmond Tutu

The stories Hannah shares—about being invisible, ashamed, and exploited—cracks open the hearts and minds of others. It has happened around the world as she steps onto stages and speaks to thousands … and it has happened in my very own living room.

Recently, she visited Denver. A dear friend of mine had spent the evening listening to Hannah's story, and in just one evening, human trafficking shifted from that of a distant cause to something deeply personal, through Hannah's eyes and voice. My friend was broken open. She woke up. Overcome with grief, she sobbed her way home, pounding the steering wheel at the injustice done to Hannah, her community, and many millions around the globe.

And, right then and there, in the midst of her weeping, she sensed a question in her heart: *Why have you never cried or pounded the steering wheel for the injustice you suffered? You and Hannah are not so different. Your body was mistreated and abused sexually, too. Your heart was broken from the pain that you've not fully felt.*

My friend shared this intimate moment of epiphany with me. "What Hannah's story did was break down a barrier in my heart around my own childhood sexual abuse. When I connected with Hannah, I was moved for the first time in my life to look at, feel, and begin to heal from this trauma. I've been in therapy for decades, but I've never spoken of this—I've always been too ashamed of it. But, when I saw Hannah's healing, I was filled with hope that the same is possible for me."

My friend's personal struggle has been great, but she wasn't able to face it, acknowledge it, and weep over it *until she heard Hannah's story.*

Without a doubt, Hannah is a leader, a COURAGEous warrior of love. She inspires and awakens that courage in others. She has ignited not only the women of Nepal, but countless others with her passion to set the world ablaze with hope. Today, Hannah is free, dancing her way through life, whirling around the world, sharing stories and inviting us to join her as sisters and brothers, to flood the dark places in the world with light, together.

Hope's Glow

HOPE IS NEEDED AND IT IS FLOURISHING AROUND THE WORLD, IN NEIGHBORHOODS, VILLAGES, REFUGEE CAMPS, AND WAR ZONES.

For me, at the peak of my eating disorder and during other everyday human struggles, hope was there. I was never alone.

Even when I couldn't see hope or my companions clearly through my squinting, tired eyes, it flickered. Even when I couldn't hear, feel, or sense much of anything good, hope was alive. At those times, the world—and my life—seemed so very, very dark. But even in the midst of those dim days, there was a spark that never went out, a nudge not to give up that was lodged in my heart. Hope was glowing beyond what I could see. It sat right next to, within, and around the struggle and pain.

> The fear, darkness, and struggles that are in the world or within you may be massive, but they are trumped by love and light and hope—always.

Do you feel it, do you see it too? Are addiction, brokenness, and pain present in your own life and in the lives of those you love? Do you feel bits or a bunch of shame, fear, sorrow, and darkness within and around you? Does the unimaginable injustice in the world seem greater than the hope? Does it seem that nightmares are stronger than dreams?

Within the struggle, the pain, the broken—even before you see or feel it—hope is present. Take heart and know the struggle will not last forever. Sometimes hope is particularly hard to see, but it is there. The fear, darkness, and struggles that are in the world or within you may be massive, but they are trumped by love and light and hope—always.

pop

6 Be Still (surrender)

In the pain, pause.
In the heartbreak, pause.
Whether you feel a flicker of hope or feel nothin', pause.
Breathe deep, full, big breaths.
Breathing in hope.
Breathing in love. Breathing in peace.
Stay here for a few more minutes.

ponder (go deeper)

Listen to "Glory," sung by John Legend and Common.
This is a song of freedom, of dignity, of fighting for justice
with others ... a movement of many. Listen for the themes
of everyday people doing their part.

Where are the flickers of hope in the world and in your
own heart? How might you stoke the fire of hope, of
beauty, even in the hard—even in the pain—in your life
challenges or challenges in the world that you are aware
of?

Take whatever feels hopeless in or around you. Really
think about it. Imagine it. What does it look, sound, feel
like? Imagine a glow of some goodness entering into the
hopelessness ... a light, a seed planted and growing,

a song of beauty, a shout of truth, a small act with great love. Invite Spirit to be there and to plant in you a seed of hope today. In your way with your voice, write about and ask for a glimpse or a sense of hope's glow. Even if you feel nothing exceptional right now, be expectant. Be watchful.

Engage (commit)

A nudge. Reach out to one person today who needs a bit of hope's glow. A stranger or a friend. Someone near or far.

Now, it's your turn. What or who are you beckoned to *commit to, connect with*, or *create*—whether in small or big ways?

Share something from this PoP with someone you trust.

BE BOLD. BE BRAVE. BE YOU.

3

[sparking]

glimmering. inspiring. activating or inciting. setting off a sudden force.

one-of-a-kind

You are here with a destiny that is
one-of-a-kind in nature.
There's no one like you—never has been,
never will be.
This is your superPOWER.
Open up to the truth, claim it, share it.

Until you express your one-of-a-kind destiny
in thought, word, and deed,
the world will not see or benefit
from its stunning gift.

When you do, you will be living
—really living—
in that edge-of-your-seat sort of a way.

Waiting for You

LIVING A LIT UP, SPARKING LIFE, NEED NOT BE DEPENDENT ON KNOWING AND SEEING CLEARLY THE PATH FORWARD.

It does not require you to wholly understand your gifts, your destiny, or your why. It is not dependent upon a sense of potent proficiency. Perhaps this is the most *needed nudge* thus far.

A deeply natural and exceedingly common human tendency is to believe that living with good juju of feelings like joy, peace, and confidence requires lots of other accomplishments first. But it's not true. This way of life is not *out there* in the future or dependent on you doing anything first. A full-to-the brim experience of a daily life *sparking* with feel-good meaning and purpose can be yours here and can be part of your daily life now, in the midst of the not-yet-known, the not-yet-understood, and the not-yet-proficient. You can walk through life, your head held high with confidence, even amidst these not-yet bits.

This is good news. Your value, your worth, and your purpose are planted in you. They reside in you. They are yours. Right here and right now.

If you don't know your exact next steps, your whys, your hows, or your whats, not to worry. They're coming. When you see your next step, take it. Know that it will be unique to you. The ways you decide to express what you want to do and how you want to do it will look different from other people's. Thank goodness.

I have treasured friends I deeply love and respect, who work and live around the United States in *EVERYday*, extraordinary ways of life, expressing a prismatic diversity of service. I'd like to introduce you to some of them. They are a testament to the myriad ways we can take our next steps, even in the midst of sickness, jobs, and family ... the real bits and pieces that come with being human.

> Your value, your worth, and your purpose are planted in you. They reside in you. They are yours.

Anna is a momma of three, an artist, and an entrepreneur. Her much-loved dad was recently diagnosed with cancer; she often heads to the hospital to sit with him during his treatments. After one of the treatments, she sent this note about her day with him: "I have had the opportunity to help other cancer patients while with my dad, whether they need a warm blanket or lunch from the cafeteria—it has been a joy for me to help these people in need. I sat with a little grandma last time, and she wept to me about how scared she is to know she is dying. I held her hand and tried to comfort her."

Dom is a surf coach, bringing insight about life and world events through conversations and fostering a rich perspective about our global *ohana* (Hawaiian for "family") as he rises and falls on the waves with his students.

Nicole works for a large corporation and is fired up with a dream to create a platform for increased access to medical records so that patients can understand and advocate for what they need. Her eyes sparkle and her voice elevates as she talks about her passion for this work.

Momma Sue, my mother-in-law, is fueled by a gigantic passion to make memories with our family. She spends her days in extravagant love and support of her mom, who is also her roommate and best friend (our beloved, sassy, and wise Nana). She is also a formidable leader in her tribe, a mighty and merry group of widows.

Pat, my dad, is a retired doctor who is part of a team of volunteers who have created a free mobile health clinic in their community, offering healthcare to refugees who cannot yet afford health insurance. He masterfully builds bridges and *comPASSIONATEly* extends fundamental healthcare support to those in great need.

Lisa quit her day job as a social worker and now weaves her passion for social justice and fashion and has created Stylish Sparrow (stylishsparrow.com), a visionary social enterprise. This company impacts lives locally and globally through building community, and educating about fair trade, human trafficking, child labor, *and* the dignity of a life in which women feel comfortable in their skin, wearing clothes that fully express who they are.

Each one of these cherished friends is making a mighty difference in the midst of their work, their families, and their neighborhoods … within their everyday lives. They are a reminder that living your purpose on the planet is not necessarily about making massive changes, quitting your day job, and traveling to distant places to live or visit. It is more about reorienting your focus, attention, and gaze to listen to your life as it is now.

> Each one melds what they love with whom they love and has created innovative and inspired offerings to the world that make life better.

Each one melds *what* they love with *whom* they love and has created innovative and inspired offerings to the world that make life better. They have said yes to a step or two that is creating permeating and powerful purpose within their lives. They have each found a place of belonging and a place to be themselves.

But I get it. It's complicated. The path isn't always clear. The dots can be difficult to connect. Lisa, of Stylish Sparrow, talks about the struggle she felt for years as she tried to integrate and understand the ways in which she might fuse her passion for fashion and social justice. She shares, "They seemed to be irreconcilable. I felt stifled in my attempts to move in the direction of building a business around fashion, as it seemed so superficial and unimportant in the face of things that 'really mattered.'" But, in the midst of the quandaries, the unknown, and the discomfort, our remarkable sister Lisa kept walking, one *COURAGEous* step at a time. Step by step, she has created something absolutely remarkable that is profoundly impacting those near and far.

That's all we can do. Step by step ... keep walking.

So, my friend, keep walking. Don't give up. Don't lose heart. Don't quit. Keep cultivating places where you can *be* yourself, claim your unique passions and purpose, find ways to collaborate with others, and boldly build these rhythms of taking time to fuel yourself from deep within.

Step by step, it will make a difference. You will feel good and do good. This way of life will become as effortless as the thrumming of your heart.

Treasure Hunt

TREES WHISPER. A BREEZE BLOWS. I AM SIX YEARS OLD. MY AUNT DEBY AND I ARE HAVING AN OUTDOOR TEA PARTY. (YES, THE SAME BELOVED AUNT MENTIONED EARLIER.)

We wear floppy hats, sip tea, and imagine we are in England, at the palace with the queen. Her pretend British accent lilts and tickles my ears. It is the first memory I have of an accent, and right then and there, I am captivated.

As I grew, so did my curiosity and passion to surround myself with people from all around the world. I posted *National Geographic* pictures and world maps on my walls in my childhood bedroom. They hung from my ceiling and covered my door. These images were of distant lands and communities—of food, homes, and villages I'd not yet seen. I would go to sleep and wake up thinking about these people and places. Even then—in my early days of life—I dreamt that I would see, visit, eat with, and get to know these strangers in distant lands.

Years later, as a teenager, I was offered the extraordinary opportunity to go to India. I basked in the sounds of new languages and blaring horns I heard as I got off the plane in Calcutta, the wave of hot air that hit my skin as I exited the airport, the sensation of wearing saris, the mode of traveling around the city in rickshaws, the smells of aromatic spices coming from the street food vendors at every corner, and the *deLIGHT* to my senses of steaming, sweet, spicy, and milky chai.

One afternoon, I headed outside with a friend, in the midst of my first monsoon. We walked into warm sheets of rain plunging from the sky and watched the streets swell from puddles to streams to rivers. Shopkeepers moved with focused and accustomed determination, effortlessly and expediently clanging their shop doors down within minutes to protect their wares. I muffled a scream as a mouse trying to escape the flooding streets ran across my toes, the first of many firsts in this far-off land.

> **This bewildering familiarity and joy were clues pointing to my purpose.**

From the very start, I felt at home. Back then, it was a bit of a mystery. I found myself thinking, *How can it be, that a place so unfamiliar, so different, feels like home?* But, now, I know why. I understand. This bewildering familiarity and joy were clues pointing to my purpose.

I fell in love with the posse of kids who begged for money on India's streets, trailing me with eyes pleading to give them something of value. I'd tucked pieces of gum in my pockets to offer and blew bubbles as I walked. I loved sitting down with them, tousling their hair, giving hugs, and smiling a warm hello.

Over a ginger-spiced cup of chai one afternoon, I sat across from Christy, a friend who had been living in India for ten years. When I told her about my encounters with the kids on the street, she gently asked me if I knew that many of them had been unimaginably mistreated, purposefully handicapped, burned, blinded, and undernourished. She explained, "Those who own or have power over them have figured out that sick, thin, and disabled kids generate more money than do the healthy. This is the reality throughout India and in many parts of the world among the vulnerable poor."

My thoughts collided, violently tumbling over one another. *What? Nooooo way! Wait, how can this be? This was done to them?* My brain shorted out with incomprehension. Time stopped. My tears poured into my chai. My head and heart ached.

I remembered seeing lots of blind children, some whose skin was badly burned, and others on wheeled platforms, scooting from one place to another, their limbs twisted or missing. Blowing bubbles and sharing a piece of gum suddenly felt terribly inconsequential and paltry. I was humbled at the smallness of my offerings in the face of this reality.

The next morning, I headed out to make my way through the streets. However, I walked and looked around differently. I still handed out gum and blew bubbles, but did so with a palpable ferocity that had begun to burn in me. I didn't want to look the other way or to shrink away from the heartbreak.

A seed of a dream was planted in me on that hard and humble walk. It beckoned me to commit to be a part of life with those who are vulnerable to this sort of cruel exploitation. That seed has grown since then, its roots deepening and becoming an inextricable part of my passion to do my part whenever I can with and for these bright-eyed beauties.

Many years later, I met a remarkable woman, Jaimala, who has become a treasured soul sister. She wrote a book, *Eighteen Million Question Marks*, about the millions of vulnerable kids who live on the streets of India. A fierce visionary and innovative force of love, she co-founded Vatsalya (vatsalya.org), an organization that cares for these resilient and at-risk kids. In the desert of Jaipur, India, she has crafted an oasis of a community-family, breathtaking in beauty, love, and fresh starts, radiant with possibilities for these wee ones.

My days with Jaimala and her cherished children in the desert of Jaipur grew that seed, first planted in my teens, and fueled the fire that was building in me. 'Cuz that's what happens in this mighty tribe. Our sparks kindle the flame in one another. Over and over.

I see how that passion was being sparked and stoked years earlier, in my first memory of an accent with Aunt Deby … as I ripped out magazine pages and wallpapered my room with people and life from all over the world … when I got on a plane bound for India as a teenager … and as I sipped and cried an ocean of tears into my chai with Christy. Such simple, *EVERYday*, and important clues for the treasure hunt of my life. Step by step, year by year, the sparks would be set more ablaze, the distance would lessen, and these faraway people and I would connect and claim one another as family.

> Step by step, year by year, the sparks would be set more ablaze, the distance would lessen, and these faraway people and I would connect and claim one another as family.

What's in a name?

SOMETIMES YOU CAN LOOK TO WHAT HAS BEEN GIVEN TO YOU, WHAT YOU DIDN'T CHOOSE, AND FIND HINTS THAT WILL INFORM AND EXPRESS WHO YOU ARE, MAYBE EVEN UNCOVERING A BIT MORE OF WHAT MATTERS TO YOU.

My name is one of those things. Although I didn't choose it, much of what I love and clues to my destiny are portrayed in mine: Sarah Jane Davison-Tracy[-Badi]. Each word offers a glimpse of my heartbeat and connections that pulse with purpose.

Sarah means "princess of God." My identity has been rooted and grown in the presence of this One who is closer to me than my breath and who guides me each step of the way. Here, I am lavishly loved and empowered, whether in the public or private spheres. When I experience the security of this identity, I live *footloose and fancy free*, and more importantly, I am able to more *BOLDly* express who I am with confidence. I am a humble and fierce warrior in more of life each day.

My godmother, *Jane*, taught me about the ways in which storytelling is a crucial part of community life, as it is here that we have the opportunity to remind each other of the good and the true, both now and in years past. Living just two houses down from us, it was as if her front door was always unlocked just for me to burst through whenever I wished. Jane's four children were my second set of siblings; she and her husband, Bill, remain two of my most treasured elders. There is no doubt: I am who I am, in part, because of this family, and in them, my love of the village was born.

Davison is my husband's family name. In our days of engagement, as Brandon and I envisioned and made plans for our life *together*, even then, I knew that words—our names—mattered. I very much wanted an external reflection of the vows we were about to take, so I asked Brandon to consider changing his name when we married. I was eager to start our life together with a significant change that reminded us that *together* we were different. Of course, in those days of courtship, I had no idea how these differences would at times dangerously divide us and ultimately become the secret ingredient in the mortar holding our partnership together.

My maiden name, *Tracy*, is a good ol' Irish name. It speaks to my early roots of tribe. My parents were my first elders, and they are so very wise. They are courageous pilgrims, evidencing robust faith, radical trust, and fierce commitment in life. And my two remarkable sisters gave me my first taste of the joy that soul sisters bring. We have grown together, as a tribe of three, over the years.

We have not been an idyllic bunch in which it has always been easy and pretty to be a Davison or a Tracy. Far from it. Some seasons have found our family to be mighty messy, with individual or relational challenges aplenty. In it all, it has been breathtaking to see the glimmers of beauty that have emerged out of our struggles. Our twofold *Davison-Tracy* name is a real-life reminder of the ways in which hope and healing are possible, no matter how broken something is.

In essence—albeit not legally—my final last name is *Badi*. This name has its roots in a memorable walk on a dusty, breezy, 110-degree blazing hot day. I was with two friends, Hannah and Sarita, wandering through their village in the far west of Nepal. As we walked, their families and friends called us over, beckoning us to sit with them on each of their front porches. I knew about their challenges in my head. But that smokin'-hot day, I saw their difficulties anew, as I sat on their porches with them and listened to their heartbreak.

As I've shared a bit already, they have struggled as a people in unimaginable ways. I listened to stories of the not-enough-ness of poverty, illness, missing and trafficked children, and gut-wrenching hardship for so many. Yet, their problems were not the ultimate focus or the end of the story.

> We can do this, as a tribe and family. We can grow one another: new names, identities, and stories beckon.

Their stories of lament were interspersed with singing and speaking about the ways in which all was not lost. One after the other evidenced sparking hope in the midst of the hardship.

As we headed back to join Hannah's family on her front porch, Hannah took my hand in hers, drawing us to a stop. With tears in her eyes, she thanked me for coming to her village, for listening, for walking, for being with her neighbors and her family—with those she loves. She then gave me my newest last name. "Sarah *didi* (which means "sister" in Nepali)," she said, "You are now one of us. You are a Badi. Your name is now Sarah Badi." Just like that, I grew. Hannah expanded my name—expanded me— that day.

We can do this, as a tribe and family. We can grow one another: new names, identities, and stories beckon.

▶ 7 *Be Still (surrender)*

Yes, new things await.
New things are here.
But, for now, let them go.
For now, be still.
Stay here, for as many moments as you can spare.

ponder (go deeper)

Listen to "Love Rescue Me," sung by U2. Also, find and listen to the fantastic version by the Omagh Community Youth Choir. This song speaks about being without a name, of shame, and conquering the past. It invokes new beginnings. *Ponder* and write about the words and rhythms meant for you.

What hints can you gather from the places you came from, from the people you have lived with—those who have loved you or those who have caused you pain? What clues can you glean from your name that speak to your purpose? What hints does your name give you as to what matters to you? Write a bit about how your name expresses who you are.

Are there names you call yourself or ways your identity is smaller, more limiting, not quite suiting who you know yourself to be? In my spiritual tradition, there are many stories in which God gives a new name to one who is in need of an identity change. If this draws you in, spend some time in dialogue with the Sacred, walking, writing, or listening for a divinely-inspired name change.

Engage (commit)

A nudge. Have a conversation with someone you trust today, someone who has known you for a long time, and ask them to share their insights about what they see as intrinsic aspects of you. Write down and ponder a bit what they share. What excites you? What intrigues you?

Now, it's your turn. What or who are you beckoned to commit to, connect with, or create—whether in small or big ways?

Share something from this PoP with someone you trust.

BE BOLD. BE BRAVE. BE YOU.

gathering momentum

Your heart, right now, is beating.
— thrum, thrum, thrum —
It just happens,
effortlessly.
It is — you are — pulsing with life.

My heart quickens now.
— thrum, thrum —
imagining you at this point in your jOURney,
connecting more wholly
with your mighty human family.

Some are near, others far.
Some speak your tongue,
others speak different languages.
In the midst of all that is distinctively different,
we are inextricably interconnected.
— thrum, thrum —

Riding the Wave

I ACCIDENTALLY FELL IN LOVE WITH SURFING A FEW YEARS AGO WHEN I STUMBLED ON A LITTLE-KNOWN AND AMAZING SURF BREAK WHILE ON A RETREAT. IT REMAINS ONE OF THE HAPPIEST ACCIDENTS OF MY LIFE.

Rising and falling with the waves awakened something in me. It makes my heart sing. I can be and I can play; I am just plain happy in the sea.

It has nothing to do with being good at it, because—*ahem*—I am *not* good … *yet*. Living in landlocked Colorado has made for ocean moments that are few and far between. A big dream of mine is to live, one day, in a warm place on a surf break, beginning and ending each day in the water and riding in those iconic barrels of a wave.

Over and over, I have received numerous nuggets of insight from surf instructors. What they have shared with me has profoundly impacted and informed my life … on and off my board. In Costa Rica, my buddy Helberth has been surfing since he learned to walk. I love this *hermano* (Spanish for "brother"). He offers simple—and *not* easy—insights in between surf sets. His wise words would often send me scrambling to write them down in my journal at the end of our *sesh*, before I forgot them. The two nuggets that have stuck with me the most are these:

Mira a donde quieres ir.
Look where you want to go.

Pare el momento.

Stop the moment.

Insight one: Look where you want to go. *Mira a donde quieres ir.* It remains one of my greatest and most empowering learning curves. It challenges me to keep my vision fixed on where I want to go (not at what I fear), as I paddle for and *pop-up* to ride the gleaming wall of water.

As the wave barrels towards me, formidable with force, it sometimes casts a shadow on me. In that moment, there are many things that need to happen simultaneously in my muscles, mind, and balance in order for me to surf a wave. If fear and overwhelm take over in this moment, my natural inclination is for my gaze to become riveted on the bottom of the wave. When that happens, even before I try to ride it, I've lost. It is *no bueno* (Spanish for "no good"). When I've focused there, I have wiped out and found myself under the wave, where I am tossed to and fro in that churning and often violent tumult. The bottom of the wave is *not* where I want to go. I want to ride and be carried by the energy of the wave instead of being crushed by it. To do so, it's *simple.* I need my vision to be *simply focused*, to sweep up and across to the face of the wave. It is there where *I want to go*, to pop-up on my board, gracefully ride, and playfully practice until the wave fades into the effervescent whitewater.

Mira a donde quieres ir. This is also a "right on," powerful message for this part of our journey. *Tick tock.* The time is now to *look where you want to go.* Even when—especially when—there is a bunch of big energy, loud noise, deep shadows, and other distractions coming at you. The more you practice, the easier it will be. See yourself *graceFULLY* gliding down the wave of life with greater finesse and ease as you focus on where you want to go.

Insight two: Stop the moment. *Pare el momento.* On my surfboard, if I freak out in the midst of my steep learning curve and if overwhelm overtakes me, I become rigid, unfocused, and incapable of doing what I want to do. It is tempting and oh, so natural, to feel stressed in the midst of the sensory stimuli of a lot of things happening at once. But if—in the midst of the wave's shadow, feeling the rise as it initially lifts me, within the very real and messy learning curve of how to ride this wave—I can *pare el momento,* take a beat, breathe, look around, and look where I want to go, magic happens. *Everything changes.* My muscles relax. My face softens. My brow unfurrows. My mouth turns up with a smile. It is more fun. I am *peaceFULL.* And the bonus: I have a way better shot at actually riding the wave.

> Tick tock. The time is now to look where you want to go.

Pare el momento. The ten PoPs within these pages are grounded in this wisdom. Whether you feel overwhelmed, fearful, and messy in your learning curves or you're rockin' and rollin' down the wave of life with skill and strength, *stopping the moment* is about creating robust rhythms in the midst of the realities of life here and now.

I remember one morning when Helberth suggested I try something new. "*Sarita* (Spanish for "Princess"), why don't you try to switch up your stance on the board?" Moving between your right and left foot as the source of powerful leading on the surfboard is called *switchfoot. Hmm, sounds fun,* I thought. I've since learned that all kinds of fantastic things—versatility, balance, and flexibility—come with practicing switchfoot on a board. But the first few times I tried it, I experienced none of those things. I was sloppy and terribly awkward. It seemed virtually impossible. I'm still not able to switchfoot with finesse and grace.

There are times when I play with the idea of *switchfooting* in my day-to-day life and challenge myself to shift from what's comfortable, what's easier, and how I've always done it, to something new.

There are times when I play with the idea of *switchfooting* in my day-to-day life and challenge myself to shift from what's comfortable, what's easier, and *how I've always done it*, to something new. For many years, my source of *powerful leading* was in *doing*. Doing was my primary *stance* as I surfed through life.

If I neglect regular rhythms of PoPs, I get overly rigid in this doing. I find myself on a frenetic hamster wheel. I stay up too late at night and get up too early in the morning. There is little rest and few moments of pause. My brow becomes furrowed, my gut gets tight, and my movements become too rapid. I overschedule myself and leave little-to-no margin to *be*. Here, the messages to *try harder* and *not enough* prevail.

When I don't switchfoot out of this stance, I wipe out. Hard. It's only a matter of time.

Wipeouts are no fun, but they sure can teach me—when I am open to listening. The nuggets have been plentiful and rich over the years …

"Wait. Slow down. Stop the moment."
"You don't have to try so hard."
"Relax. Let go a bit."
"Breathe."

"Be still."
"Don't try to do this alone."

These game-changing nuggets of wisdom are always found within my PoPs and from my tribe. Each and every time I reach out to my tribe after a wipeout, they pick me up and cheer for me to keep on going ... even when I feel I've got nothin'—or worse, that I *am* nothin'. I find that my need to strive diminishes. I often hear a whisper of next steps, and the flames of hope spark. I'm fueled more by love and less by fear. With more love, the *DOing* is different. *Life is good* in this place.

This particular switchfoot has resulted in more-than-ever freedom and soul-rest in my life. It has also been an exceptional time-management tool, as I am more discerning about when and to what I say yes. It has fostered great clarity in my work, has deepened my marriage, and has expanded my vision for motherhood.

> You have great worth. You are valuable. You are loved because of who you are, not because of what you do. Bask in it and believe it.

Yes, this switchfooting is powerful stuff, a force for feel-good change. So, my friend, if you are inclined to overdo, if you find yourself pressed, often running late or up too late, try this switchfoot and be still a bit more. Watch for patterns in your thoughts and actions that tell you the more you do, the more valuable you are. This is one of the biggest and most destructive messages in our human experience. *Switchfoot* it and be free of that burdensome belief.

You have great worth. You are valuable. You are loved because of who you are, not because of what you do. Bask in it and believe it.

Opening the Floodgates

RAISE YOUR VOICE AND SHOUT AN EXUBERANT YES! TO YOUR UNIQUE WAYS TO BE AND DO.

See new ways to give, serve, and connect with those around you. Uncover and offer your one-of-a-kind gift to those near and far. Share and listen to stories. Take little or big steps. Move with *bistari* and cultivate robust rhythms in your PoPs.

Tend to what is capturing your attention in the struggles of those in your common human family. Explore what is your brave and wholehearted response. As you do, watch for it: the floodgates of *comPASSION* will open. They just will.

> To be compassionate is to have a heart that suffers from the misfortune of others because we think of it as our own. We are truly compassionate when we work to remove the misfortune of others. The love of neighbor requires that not only should we be our neighbor's well-wishers, but also their well-doers.
> -Thomas Aquinas

You will celebrate differences anew and increase your capacity to love in thought, word, and deed. This shift will be surprising in scope, touching your family, next-door neighbors, good friends whose hearts are breaking ... and expand to those far away.

When you are present, with eyes wide open to those around you, you embrace a shared humanity of belonging, *grateFULLY* contemplate your gifts, and eagerly look for opportunities to share what is yours. Here, you are not striving or *trying harder*, but something better moves you.

Compassion is a colossally compelling force.

Take some time to ask—and listen—to compassion's beckoning. Stay rooted in the day-to-day realities of your life. Look for places of inspiration and clarity about what matters most to you.

These clues for your next steps will be there. I have a hunch they are here right now. Sometimes you just need to pause, adjust your focus, and look in order to find them.

Ruffling Our Feathers

THERE ARE THINGS THAT WHEN WITNESSED, YOU RESPOND TO AUTOMATICALLY, INSTINCTIVELY. YOU JUST DO. YOU CAN'T NOT.

If you were to see a child running into a busy street with cars whipping by in rush-hour traffic, you would likely not need to force yourself to shout or do everything possible to reach the little one.

You would do what you could in that moment, likely without a great deal of over-thinking. You would act. *You couldn't not.*

Deepening your belief that you are inextricably interconnected with those in your vast human family transforms your thoughts, your heart, and what you do. Deepening your conviction that those near and far in your human family belong to you and you to them changes the way you see the global realities of poverty, slavery, and exploitation. It becomes nearly impossible to look away.

You can't stand by. You won't stand by. *You won't do nothing.*

My kids have been learning—and in turn, teaching me—about this for years. At school, they are immersed in a community of difference-makers. They tell me about what they are learning regarding the daily choices a person has to make to be a by-stander or upstander. These two mindsets are markedly different. A *bystander* is a person who sees someone being mistreated and doesn't do anything. Maybe they look the other way. Their reasons for doing nothing could be because they're afraid, they're in a rush to get to where they're going, or they don't think they are big enough to do anything. These commonplace human pressures lure kids on the playground and adults alike to rush by and look away.

> The trouble is that once you see it, you can't unsee it. And once you've seen it, keeping quiet, saying nothing, becomes as political an act as speaking out. There's no innocence. Either way, you're accountable.
> -Arundhati Roy,
> Power Politics

Instead, my kids tell me how they are encouraged to look for op-portunities to be *upstanders*. Essentially, an upstander is someone who *wades into the troubles* of their classmates by offering com-panionship, sticks with them during hard moments, and supports them however they are able. Sometimes this means standing next to a peer who is telling their story. At other times, it involves get-ting help from a teacher if the situation seems to be bigger than a kid can handle alone.

Simple. And *simply relevant* to what is needed across the planet.

Admittedly, there are times in my life when I'm not an upstander. The difficulty may seem too distant, occurring in a different part of town or halfway around the globe from me. At other times, I see a struggle or injustice, but I look away, because it is too scary, too dark, and too hard to take in—or I don't think there is a way I can make a meaningful difference.

It can be overwhelming and gut-wrenching to see the injustice. Yet, it also feels awful to do nothing, to just stand by or pass by, doing nothing.

Good. I say, *good*. It's *good* that we feel tightness in our jaws or nagging discomfort when we do nothing, pretend, pass by, or walk away. It's *good* that the problem is too big for us to tackle alone and propels us to reach out for our tribe to find ways, together, to do something.

Allowing this very discomfort has changed me in many *EVERY*day ways. In the city in which I live, there are many who stand on street corners, holding signs and asking for help. The less I see these folks as "strangers," the less often I zip off and look away without pausing and doing something … even a *small something*. If I'm on a phone call, I may pause, smile, and wave. Sometimes I make a cup of coffee or hot chocolate to take on the way to school. If I have nothing to give or it's not possible to stop, I may say a prayer of blessing.

You may wonder, "What difference does this really make, waving, smiling, praying, offering a small something in the face of an epic need such as homelessness?" I get it. These very thoughts have slowed, confused, and stopped me. But *I contest* it in my thinking. *I contest* it with everything in me that I need to be a homeless (or other "issue") expert to do something. *I contest* that only big acts matter. *I contest* insulating myself, keeping at bay uncomfortable feelings of my feathers being ruffled. And yet, there are days I want to just give up … to stop the contesting.

Maybe there have been times when you, too, have wanted to give up instead of contest. If so, it can be tempting to ignore, tolerate, or anesthetize yourself from the pain and discomfort that is present around you. And yet, there are things that beckon for your attention. There are people who beckon for your attention. It takes courage to acknowledge the places that break your heart, to humbly bow your head, observing and tending to the discomfort. This act fuels significant change in your life. I invite you to be willing to be uncomfortable and allow your feathers to be ruffled. It is possible—and essential—when you *jOURney* with your tribe. It is simple, but not easy.

Belonging is Compelling

IMAGINE, FOR A MOMENT, THAT YOU ARE WALKING ON AN EXQUISITE PATH THROUGH GENTLE ROLLING HILLS.

A gurgling creek frames one side of the path, and the beauty of the trees and flowers brings a sparkle to your eyes and a smile to your lips. As you wind around the bend, you come upon a large pool, deep blue in color.

Above, a waterfall cascades and glitters in the sun as it plunges into the waters below, soothing your ears with the sounds of its tumbling. You slide off your sandals and dip your toes into the cool water. You lie back and close your eyes, taking it all in as you let your feet dangle at the water's edge. You bask in the beauty of this moment. *Ahh, life is good.* You needed this.

A breeze brushes against your skin and brings with it the faint sound of music, laughter, and a delectable whiff of food cooking. Stomach rumbling and your curiosity piqued, you pull your feet out of the water, tuck your sandals back on, and wander inquisitively toward what you smell and hear.

As you round the bend, you see a lavish table set in a grove of trees. In the approaching dusk-light, candles flicker in lanterns hung among tree limbs that sway in the breeze. You're drawn into the lovely scene and the mystery of what you've come upon.

Voices call to you. "Hey there! Hi … c'mon and join us!" You walk over, and in no time, you are swept into a festive crowd of welcoming strangers, folded into the circles of energetic discussions. Scents waft and conversations flow easily. There is much laughter … and a sense of great ease.

In a few moments, it is time to eat. You join the many others and take a seat at the table. This table is extraordinary, more than a bit magical. As you look down the length of it, to the left and right, you discover that it has no end. It curves 'round bends, down into valleys, up and over hills. There is ample room for everyone. There are empty place settings waiting to be filled. Languages, yet unfamiliar to you, are being spoken. There are many people from many places feasting at this table.

There is an element of deep respect and thoughtfulness for one another, but it is not stuffy with pretense of "proper" conversation or manners. People eagerly eat new foods and try new utensils of fingers and cutlery. It's a bit messy and delightfully relaxed. The topics of dialogue do not center only on easy days and comfortable places. Some share stories of unimaginable struggle and cruelty. Tears of anger and disappointment fall, hands clasp across the table, heads bow, and prayers are whispered. And yet, amongst the difficult and inconceivable stories, there are ample tales of good news. In the midst of the hard, hope sparks.

> **This connection with people *you call your own* changes things—it will change you.**

You notice pockets of people strategizing ideas for how to respond to the challenges. It is palpable here: these epic needs can be addressed, but only *together*. They are too vast, too inconceivable, too complex, to explore solo. You know it and feel it. They must—and they can be—responded to, but only *together*.

Sitting and sharing at this table expands your thinking about your part in the stories of those around you. You join the conversation, sometimes listening and sometimes speaking. You are surprised to be more open and eager than ever to participate with these many others.

My dear friend, even as you read and imagine this feast … blend in a bit of a PoP. Here and now, consider the part you are destined to play in it all, because you have a vital part. Move beyond your comfort zone. Fall in love more and more with your mighty human family. This connection with people *you call your own* changes things—it will change you. It will open the door for you to unleash more of who you are. It will fan the flame of your one-of-a-kind purpose on the planet.

You will discover more of who you are and what matters most to you. You were made for this. You were made to witness with wonder what grows when you plant your little or big seeds alongside your unstoppable tribe.

You won't stop. You can't. You won't want to.

Perhaps you have been overwhelmed in the past by the plethora of causes or issues that come your way … maybe in a nonstop flood of needs or in a burdensome message that you "*should* do more for others.*" You may have been burned out with your attempts to respond to such issues in the past. But this is different. The world's challenges, problems, epidemics, and systems of injustice are not so much about *issues*; these issues are really about *people*.

When what you do becomes more focused on *who instead of what*— people instead of *issues*—things change in a big way. At the heart of these issues so often spoken about in the news and in conversation are *people*: mothers, fathers, children, grandparents, brothers, and sisters.

> If to be feelingly alive to the sufferings of my fellow-creatures is to be a fanatic, I am one of the most incurable fanatics ever permitted to be at large.
> -William Wilberforce, slave-trade abolitionist

They are people with flesh—with legs, arms, eyes, eyelashes, and fingernails. They are people with laughter and longing, dreams and desires.

The purpose and power of this way of seeing one another is that it forges a *compelling connection* that changes your thinking and actions alike. You—we—become *bound by belonging.*

The boundaries of this belonging are limitless, stable, and connected. This belonging exists between and within countries, races, classes, genders, castes, and on and on. It transforms your thinking and your actions … with those nearest and furthest, most similar and most different.

As a global human family, this is our moment to stop seeing one another as separate, as other, as strangers.

As a global human family, *this is our moment* to stop seeing one another as separate, as *other*, as strangers. *This is our moment* to stop looking away. *This is our moment* to stop waiting for someone else to do something. *This is our moment* to stop wishing for someone who we deem more capable or wealthy, someone who seems to have more time, to step up and do something. Our brothers and sisters in our family around the world need us and *we need them*. Many face unimaginable struggle and they feel alone. *This is our moment* to wake up and light it up.

▶8 Be Still (surrender)

Imagine the perfectly contented feeling at the end of a meal. Good drink, good food. Life is good. Stay here in that sensation and feeling. Be at peace. Be at rest. Be.

ponder (go deeper)

Listen to "Can't Hold Us," sung by Macklemore and Ryan Lewis, featuring Ray Dalton. This is a pumping poetry-song of getting out of bed with profuse purpose and energy, of bringing your superpower of one-of-a-kind juju to the world, and of unstoppably rockin' life together. You might want to get up and move around for this one. If you do, it might be a more breathless pondering and writing sesh of what captured your attention in this song. Just for fun, see if you like the "official music video."

Have you had an experience of meeting a person who deeply impacted and shifted the way you see an issue? If not, imagine how it might change the way it feels to learn about an issue by sitting with someone impacted by that "issue" over a cup of tea in your home.

Where and when have you had the experience of personally connecting with a person who, at a glance, appeared unlike you, but with whom you shared a moment of not-so-otherness and maybe of connection? When have you bumped up against or cultivated interconnection with those most vulnerable, struggling, silenced, or marginalized? If you have had an experience of either, ponder and write about them. Did it feel comfortable, uncomfortable? What did you learn? Are there any bits and pieces you want to draw into your everyday life more (or less) now?

Engage (commit)

A nudge. Take one "issue" that you are intrigued by or care about and make one personal connection around this "cause" today. Think outside the box. For example, if you care about human trafficking, reach out to a company that sells items made by people freed from trafficking and buy a birthday gift for a loved one. Or, fish around a bit to see if there are ways you can further support an organization through spreading the word on social media about what they are doing, through volunteering, or by calling them to make a *real* personal connection.

Now, it's your turn. What or who are you beckoned to *commit to, connect with,* or *create*—whether in small or big ways?

Share something from this PoP with someone you trust.

BE BOLD. BE BRAVE. BE YOU.

vocations for all

There is an energy,
a trumpet call that beckons you to rise,
to be kindled and set aglow
from within and by those around you.
Here, you will explore what I call:
vocations for all.

These vocations beckon many
—dare I say, all?—of us.
They are simple ways for you to
think, speak, and do
in the midst of your day-to-day life
of work and relationships.

Invite them to elevate, morph,
ignite your vision
for your day-to-day life
and to inform and inspire your next steps.

Warriors

THE OTHER EVENING, MY FAMILY WATCHED A BOXING MATCH. AS MUCH AS I DON'T ENJOY THE SPORT OF BOXING, THIS FIGHT GOT ME THINKING ABOUT HOW BOXING INFORMS AND ILLUMINATES ONE OF OUR COLLECTIVE'S VOCATIONS.

I began to imagine more and more of us claiming and committing to being fierce fighters, warriors of love. And I could see that it would be amazing. It would not be boring. It would not be lonely. It would be *powerFULL*.

What do you feel curious about or compelled to fight for or against? What would you train for, even to the point of exhaustion, and perhaps beyond what you feel capable of doing? Imagine what or for whom you would be willing to fight. Is it in the context of your everyday, with those you currently serve and love? Or is it about reaching out to a new someone that is capturing your attention and heart?

Do you not know your something to live or fight for yet? Are you still on the hunt? Don't compare, measure, or allow the messages that you are not enough, moving too slow, or going too fast to diminish you. Keep walking, exploring, and trusting—even before you understand it.

I've needed to do the same in many seasons. Though there are lots of things I have yet to understand about this vital vocation, I know that *I am a warrior of love*. A big part of my purpose on the planet is to fight for those in our global human family who

155

are vulnerable and who are struggling in the world due to suffocating challenges of poverty, caste, access to education, and getting their basic needs met. I am committed to fight alongside other mighty warriors who are working on behalf of our sisters and brothers living dangerously in the margins. The more I hear of their crucial strategies for the fight, the more compelled I am to find and invite more to join. Day by day, more come to join this formidable force of fierce warriors.

> My friend, to be a part of this formidable, unstoppable army, you need only claim it. You are a warrior of love.

When the dignity, security, and well-being of those who BElong to us—one or many—is being challenged, we do something. We stand up. We are upstanders. We shout. We can't not. My friend, to be a part of this formidable, unstoppable army, you need only claim it. You are a warrior of love too.

As we walk and leap together, I have found that *warrior life is rigorous*. In my life, the more fierce the fight, the more important it is to pay close attention to my *focus* and my *fuel*. One such place of discernment has been in my discovery that justice, rights, and freedom are powerful components of the pulse of my warrior heartbeat. They make my heart *thrum*, sometimes hard and fast. Propelled too predominantly without rhythms of PoPs, they distract, confuse, and exhaust. *Every time*.

Surely they are part of the fuel, yes. But in my life, when they become the principal fuel, things get upside down. I get foggy and end up fighting *against* people—instead of *for* people. Or, sometimes, I have become selfish and self-absorbed, forcing *my* way and protecting *my* domain. My motivation and movements are *off* and these important elements of my heartbeat run me into the ground and isolate me from my tribe.

In all of these vocations, but particularly with the ferocity of this warrior work, the robust rhythms of PoPs are crucial. It is where you can pay attention to things like your focus and fuel. Listen for that sometimes still, sometimes small, and always present voice of your own heart, of your tribe, and of Spirit. Discern where you are destined to go to battle and with whom. Be fueled by your purpose in the midst of the rigors of this vocation, and, most especially, as you recover and rest after a fierce fight.

> A true vocation calls us out beyond ourselves; breaks our heart in the process and then humbles, simplifies and enlightens us about the hidden, core nature of the work that enticed us in the first place. We find that all along, we had what we needed from the beginning and that in the end we have returned to its essence, an essence we could not understand until we had undertaken the journey.
> -David Whyte, *Consolations The Solace, Nourishment and Underlying Meaning of Everyday Word*

peacemakers

SHE DIDN'T HAVE THE PEACEMAKING CREDENTIALS YOU WOULD EXPECT.

She brought gifts of bubbles, balloons, and chewing gum on her peacemaking mission to Uganda. She giggled, danced, laughed, and played. She was two years old—our daughter, Sophia.

Ten years ago, our family traveled with an extraordinary group of people. For our young toddler, Sophia, whole days of travel on bumpy roads by bus were not arduous ... they were a blast. In her mind, she was escorted by a village of entertaining aunts, uncles, and grandparents, bouncing from lap to lap, playing games, reading books, chattering, and napping here and there.

Our destination was Gulu, a village in the north of Uganda, and the Internally Displaced People's (IDP) camps housing nearly two million people in post-war Uganda. Our team was there to listen to, play with, and be a part of life with a bunch of beautiful kids and their families who had been traumatized by growing up in the midst of a brutal civil war. Many were still refugees in their own country and lived in these IDP camps far away from their villages. Even as we arrived, children were missing, the panic of child soldier abductions still striking fear into the hearts of many.

> Reminding people that they are not forgotten and that they matter is peacemaking. It makes a mighty difference.

Cumulatively, our team brought a powerful array of skills to share in the areas of healthcare, art, business and community development, education, and cross-cultural engagement. Each person left an imprint, from the eldest grandfather to our two-year-old Sophia.

One day, a local leader swept Soph up into her arms and said, "Sophia, our little, yet mighty, Sophia. Do you know what you have done? You have brought hope to us. You have reminded our children that they are not forgotten, that they matter. You make them feel that way because you have traveled so far—halfway around the world—just to be with them. Sophia, you are a peacemaker."

Reminding people that they are not forgotten and that they matter is peacemaking. It makes a mighty difference.

Claim your vocation as peacemaker. Write it on the business card of your heart. Live it, not only when life is easy, but *BOLDly* when life is hard. Root your life deeper into the soil of peace in regular rhythms of PoPs, where you can connect more often and more deeply with your tribe, with your own heart, with every breath, each day.

Doing something as significant as peacemaking—here and now—is simple. It is about showing up and bringing your voice and vision to life and offering it to the world.

philanthropists

YOU HAVE GIFTS APLENTY TO GIVE THAT CAN MAKE A MIGHTY DIFFERENCE IN THE WORLD. YOU HAVE MORE THAN YOU THINK YOU HAVE THAT IS OF INEXTRICABLE VALUE TO YOU AND TO THOSE IN YOUR HUMAN FAMILY, NEAR AND FAR.

Generosity feels good. It is part of your purpose on the planet. I have seen the unspeakable joy it brings people to give what they value greatly.

I remember one such moment when a little kindergartener came up to me and gave me a baggie of pennies, quarters, dimes, a one dollar bill, little hair bows, a necklace, and a note that said, "I love you." She authoritatively charged me to take it on my next trip to Nepal and give her gift to a child on her behalf. When I leaned down and asked her about the items in the bag, she told me it contained her treasures, the things she loved most in the world. The hat of philanthropist sat squarely on the head of this wee kindergartner.

To those who may challenge this notion, let's respectfully—and heartily—disagree. Today and together, let's dispute the suggestion that philanthropy is an exclusive club only for those deemed *wealthy*. Today and together, let's dispute that the only thing that matters and makes a difference is giving in "big" ways. Instead, today and together, let's create a movement of philanthropists in which everyone is welcome and all gifts are celebrated.

I invite you to try on the hat of philanthropist. *Yes, you*. This sort of philanthropy is about an unrestrained generosity rooted in the reality of your everyday life. It finds ways to share with others the treasure trove of whatever you have and whatever you love. It elevates the way you spend your time and what you talk about with friends. It finds opportunities to travel to places and volunteer with people who captivate your heart. It makes a difference with something as ordinary as shopping, declaring that how and where you shop will be done with a commitment and connection to your sisters and brothers near and far.

> Today and together, let's create a movement of philanthropists in which everyone is welcome and all gifts are celebrated.

A few months ago, I visited a store on an errand to look for some shoes. Finding a pair I liked, I turned them over and discovered that they had been made in a country known for inhumane factories and labor practices.

I've been deeply drawn to learn about the realities of working conditions in factories around the world for some time now, and yet, there is still much I do not understand. Although it remains a confusing and complex area for me to navigate, the more I connect with stories of people—as the *causes become personal* and *shift from issues to people*—the more fierce I am to explore what my part can be.

This was one of those moments in which I knew it was time for my feathers to be ruffled. As I held those shoes in my hand, a picture popped into my mind. It was an image of a man surrounded by mountains of shoes in a factory, depicted in the film, *The True Cost* (truecostmovie.com). In that moment, it was as if the man and the mountain of shoes inserted themselves into the shoe aisle where I was standing, begging for my attention, asking me to *look* and *do something different* because of what I learned from his story. This stranger surrounded by a mountain of shoes invited me to be changed and act anew.

This film is intense. It hurts my heart to take in the stories that give evidence to the reality that around the world people work in horrific conditions, separated from their own children, weary to the bone, with no real way out of the struggle, and desperately alone. Many of these factories produce clothing, accessories, and housewares that are on the shelves of the stores I frequent. It has been uncomfortable and confusing to know my part in response to it all. And yet, despite the heartbreak, this film is one of my favorites, in great part because of Shima, one of the film's featured storytellers.

Shima Akhter is a twenty-three-year-old *COURAGEous*, intelligent, and innovative woman who lives in Bangladesh. A powerful force for change, she has empowered and unified women in her factory to fight for increased living wages and more humane working conditions. Her story has inspired me and has nudged me to reconsider my consumption of *fast fashion* clothing.

> When we commit to *BEing* and *DOing* life together, we then become part of something big. It then becomes the stuff of movements, powerfully rooted in and growing out of the everyday.

While being interviewed, there are times when Shima's eyes sparkle and other times when they tear up. Her voice trembles with emotion and a high hope for her daughter's future to be different from her own. She is ablaze with a dream. And yet, we see and hear it. Her life is hard. There are no easy answers to the massive struggles in her life and the lives of her fellow workers and family.

On that shoe aisle, on an *EVERYday* errand, I remembered the man surrounded by the mountain of shoes. I remembered Shima. I went back and forth, thinking, *Good grief, Sarah. Just buy the shoes. What difference will it make in the world—to Shima or the fella in the shoe factory—if you don't?*

Amidst the uncomfortable dissonance in me, I felt it: It was time to *switchfoot* my shopping stance into one more deeply connected to the people of the world, my human family. As I held those beautiful shoes in my hands, my throat tightened, tears filled my eyes, and I thought, *No. Not this time. Although I'm not sure if or how this makes a difference for anyone in the world, I am not going to buy these shoes today.*

In my own heart, as I walked out of the shoe store, it felt like an exhale. *Ahh, much better.* Although I was changed, did my little act have a direct bearing on the world's massive systemic challenges of unfair labor practices? No, probably not. And yet, what is less disputable is that if many of us commit to such actions—to voice what matters to us with our dollars, with our time, and in our conversations—this change will be even more likely to have an impact.

When we commit to *BEing* and *DOing* life together, we then become part of something big. It then becomes the stuff of movements, powerfully rooted in and growing out of the everyday.

My friend, this is not about shaming or guilting or piling one more burden on your shoulders. This is not about judging or affirming where you shop or talking about heady and oft' privileged notions of philanthropy. Although you and I may not see where it all will lead, this is about sitting *together, WHOLEheartedly* open to learning how to infuse more intention into our lives and to more deeply connect with and love those around us.

Hairdressers (stick with me here)

THIS COLLECTIVE VOCATIONAL NUDGE INVITES YOU TO LOOK AROUND AND SEE WHAT IS IN YOUR LIFE RIGHT NOW. RIGHT HERE AND RIGHT NOW.

What simple tools do you wield that can be shared easily with people around you—something that is connected to your job, your passion, or a way of reaching out to those around you that is easy, natural, and currently part of your everyday?

Think about something for which you don't need money, more training, or skills to be able to do. It's something you just do, and it's as easy as breathing.

As you sit with and explore this query, I have a hunch that the following story will inspire you. It is a tale of a global movement that began with a pair of hair-cutting scissors. This account of Joshua Coombes is jaw-dropping in its simplicity and *comPASSION*. Our extraordinary brother Joshua lives and works in the UK and fundamentally believes that *small acts of love greatly matter*. One day, he gathered the tools most natural and familiar to him (a stool, scissors, comb, and a razor), walked out the door of his salon in London, and began offering free haircuts to homeless people on his streets.

Joshua speaks about the roots of this committed and inspired action: "Hairdressing is how I communicate with people, but anybody, no matter who you are, can do something for nothing, make a difference in your own way. The cool thing, this can be our response to some of the world's problems. Our voice, our hands, our smile are one step away from restoring somebody's hope in humanity."

We all have tools to wield in the world akin to those of Joshua's hairdressing scissors that are simple and have the power to be a part of *restoring hope in humanity*. This is the stuff that adds ceaseless strength to the fabric of life. This is the stuff of significance and belonging. It cultivates and reveals your unique purpose on the planet.

This movement started with Joshua *seeing* the homeless on his streets as people and *looking at* the tools he had at his disposal right then and there. He connected the dots of need and his gifts.

Joshua shares that it was the nagging questions and his own sense of powerlessness that ultimately nudged him to begin.

Overwhelm didn't stop him. His destiny and next steps—just like yours—resided right next to his feelings of helplessness. He found the gold in the very place of discomfort. The struggles of home-lessness around him did not *deter* him, but *propelled* him.

As he walked, one step at a time, day after day, Joshua began capturing the attention of those around him. One by one, others have joined him. When two changemakers with gifts in compel-ling cultural "storymaking" (entrepreneur, Dave Burt, and musician, Matt Sprack-len) heard about what he was up to, they reached out to Joshua. These three gelled—they clicked. They began to do together what they could not have done solo. They now call themselves a *band of brothers* and have started a global campaign called #DoSomethingForNoth-

> This movement started with Joshua *seeing* the homeless on his streets as people and *looking* at the tools he had at his disposal right then and there. He connected the dots of need and his gifts.

ing. They say that this movement is fundamentally about linking influencers around the world through social media, spreading love around the world, and connecting the *haves* with the *have nots*.

Today, Joshua is in the salon less and traveling around the world more, speaking about this mighty global campaign with simple roots in his own backyard. Joshua's path has been uncharted and unplanned. But, one step and leap at a time, it has grown far be-yond where it was when he started on the day he picked up his hairdresser's tools and walked out his door to offer a free haircut.

Bridge-Builders

CULTIVATING A TRIBE WITHIN WHICH THERE IS PRISMATIC DIVERSITY AND COURAGEOUSLY MOVING AWAY FROM SURROUNDING OURSELVES WITH SAMENESS IS TREMENDOUSLY SIGNIFICANT AND POWERFUL.

Arms of bridge-building hospitality are powerful and far-reaching. This way of thinking and acting seeks to reach not only those who are familiar or in your comfort zone, but those who are wildly and *beautyFULLY* diverse.

It's about celebrating difference and finding places of similarity that take your breath away, filling life with more palpable purpose and connection than ever before.

In our world today, most of our political systems are split and broken and many people—regardless of nationality, race, gender, or generation—are struggling to make it through each day. The challenges you have experienced may look or sound different from another's struggles, but, oh my, we are more similar than different. I am here to offer both a gentle nudge and a caffeine-filled jolt to vehemently oppose the tendency to erect walls built by bricks of fear, shame, judgment, ignorance, distrust, and misunderstanding, to beckon you to cultivate curiosity, celebrate connection in unexpected places, and fiercely commit to honoring differences.

> It's about celebrating difference and finding places of similarity that take your breath away, filling life with more palpable purpose and connection than ever before.

Whew. That's a lot, right? And yet, it's simple. It takes us back to what my kids taught me about the difference between being an upstander and a bystander. They remind us to reach out, to not look away, and to do our part. This is the sort of wisdom wee ones have. They know this to be true. Sometimes as we grow older, we forget.

Let's *REmember* together. Here and now.

> I believe we can change the world if we start listening to one another again. Simple, honest, human conversation...Human conversation is the most ancient and easiest way to cultivate the conditions for change–personal change, community and organizational change, planetary change. If we can sit together and talk about what's important to us, we begin to come alive.
> -Margaret Wheatley,
> *Turning to One Another*

To do so now is a crucial commitment in the context of humanity, in a big global way, as well as a deeply personal one. It is rooted in the real, within the quotidian, ordinary acts of going to school, working, and raising children.

Crafting this bridge-building way of life, claiming it as one of your vocations, is one that will reorient your *gaze* and your *gifts*. It is nothing less than *REVolutionary*. Think back to the stories shared of people using their day-to-day tools to connect with, love, and serve those near and far. They are bridge-builders, each one, in unique and significant ways.

You can take on this job title, too.

You are a bridge-builder.

Every day, you encounter people and places in social media, the news, at work, in your neighborhood, and within your family that may seem strange, scary, too much *this* or not enough *that* as you go about your life. Imagine if, beginning with you, more and more people claim the work of bridge-building and

> It's about celebrating difference and finding places of similarity that take your breath away, filling life with more palpable purpose and connection than ever before.

endeavor to fiercely find ways and places to connect, despite differences and seemingly deep division. This vocation may lead you to one near and dear: your spouse, your child, a family member, friend, neighbor … or to one distant and different, due to culture, race, or religion.

As a bridge-builder, the next time you encounter a moment of difference, or of *otherness*, lean in, curiously ask questions, and really listen to and share with one another. Your thoughts, words, and actions may be distinctively different. There are infinite possibilities for ways in which your actions will ripple out and grow from you, making the world a bit brighter, a bit better.

Explorers

THE JOURNEY OF LIFE WILL BRING MOMENTS IN WHICH YOU FEEL AS THOUGH YOU ARE NAVIGATING UNCHARTED TERRITORIES. THEY WILL COME. THEY ALWAYS DO.

It can take great courage and the adventure can be thrilling. Consider that claiming the vocation of an explorer might just free you from the burden of needing to know where you are going and how you are getting there.

Rooted in Latin *explorare*, the word "explore" means to "investigate, search out, examine." Rarely, if ever, is seeing the whole path part of the quest. The exploration most often involves regions yet unfamiliar. Sometimes there are maps to consult; other times, the lands are brand new. Either way, navigating undiscovered terrains is part of the work of an explorer. It is to be expected. It is normal. Will there be unfamiliar places? Yes. Will there be unknown places? Of course. Will there be uncomfortable places? Most definitely. Though sometimes challenging, these conditions do not disqualify you; in fact, they are evidence that you are living your calling as an explorer.

Another important nudge for the road: As you continue to explore, you may or may not discover things that you deem significant. Not to worry. Keep walking. Keep exploring. Discoveries don't add to the sparkling worth of who you are.

There are always new possibilities around the bend. Keep expanding your purpose on the planet, your tribe, and the ways in which *inspired doing* lights you up. Life as an explorer has no end, and it is never hum-drum or boring. It gives you a reason to get up in the

> Keep expanding your purpose on the planet, your tribe, and the ways in which inspired doing lights you up.

morning. On some days, it takes everything you've got to stay focused and keep fueled for the rigors of life. Exploring can be hard work and can tax the body, mind, heart, and soul. You may become travel-weary in the days to come. But, my intrepid-explorer-friend, you have essentials for the road as you cultivate your own PoP practices—times to contemplate and commit to action that is fueled from deep within you. Take them with you wherever you go. They are vital and all the more crucial in rigorous days that find you traversing uncharted territories.

pop

9 Be Still (surrender)

Here we are. You may have more questions you want answered, more clarity you need, more you want to know and understand.

But, as we've done throughout this *jOURney*, in this moment, let your brow relax, your jaw loosen.

Remember this is not up to you entirely. You do not need to force, strive, or push. Let these things go. Be. Breathe.

Soften. Let go of the burdens. Open to what you most need. Just be.

ponder (go deeper)

Listen to "A Beautiful Day," sung by the amazing India Arie. This song is all about being explorers, *grateFULL-ness*, and elegant ease. *Ponder* and write about what rises within you as you listen to her song-poetry.

How might claiming this vocation of an explorer shift your expectation that you need to know everything all the time? How might it reduce your sense of worry and increase peace when you find yourself in uncharted places, in the land of the not-yet-understood?

· ·

Are there any bits of your life, whether in relationships, work, or your own clarity about your purpose on the planet, that burden you to see more clearly? *Ponder* and consider if there is another way, a lighter and freer way, to navigate uncharted and undiscovered territories.

Engage (commit)

A nudge. Commit to one thing you are most keen to explore, without the burden or pressure of needing to understand or see the whole path. One person or place or thing that is drawing you to come and see, to pay attention. Write it down. Do one thing today to be the intrepid explorer that you are.

Now, it's your turn. What or who are you beckoned to *commit to, connect with,* or *create*—whether in small or big ways?

Share something from this PoP with someone you trust.

BE BOLD. BE BRAVE. BE YOU.

4

[blazing]

being on fire. being excited.
eager. zealous. ardent. burning
brightly and with great heat.
having a force of tremendous
intensity or fever. gleaming with
bright lights, bold colors.

taking flight

It's time to leap, soar, and light up the world.
You were made for this.

This is your
—this is our—
purpose on the planet.
Hold your head high,
your eyes bright, direct, and fierce.
Grab a hand and leap BOLDly and
COURAGEously.

Leap and fly.
Live ablaze
and let's light up the world,
together.

Claim & Leap

IMAGINE THAT THIS ADVENTURE HAS BROUGHT YOU TO THE EDGE OF A CLIFF.

The vista from this vantage point is spectacular, unlike anything you've seen before. As you stand at the edge, with the parachute strapped to your back, you know it:

It is time to leap.

Your heart pounds, your breath is short. You long for the leap, to feel the wind on your skin as you fly free and unfettered. But it is not easy. You have never leapt from this height before. You know that you must jump for the 'chute to open. The terror and the thrill make for a racing heart.

Thrum-Thrum. Thrum-Thrum. Amidst the tumult of your racing heart and the whipping of the wind, something catches your eye. As you look to the left and right, you see it. It is not *something*, but *someone* … a lot of *someones*, in fact.

The cliff ledge is lined with others, and more are coming. They have been *jOURneying* and exploring, taking small and big steps, leading them to this cliff's edge. Just like you. With you.

▶10 *Be Still (surrender)*

Whew. These are audacious and exhilarating imaginings, aye? We'll return to them in a bit.

For now, my dear friend, take this time for silence and stillness. Let go of the possibilities and conundrums, the things known or unknown. Excitement or fear.

Be here. Breathing. Being.

ponder (go deeper)

Listen to (and watch the video) "Wavin' Flag — Celebration Mix," sung by K'NAAN. This is the final jam to rock to in our time together on this journey. Celebrate this final PoP. Get up and move around, dance, spin, and take in this epic and amazing connection with a tribe of many that is here for you right here and now. As you sit, sing, or dance, what is capturing your attention in this poetry-song? *Ponder* and write it down.

What are the shared vocations that beckon you to claim them, as if they are written below your name on a business card? Mark the vocations that most compel and excite you. Add ones that call to you that aren't listed here.

Dream big here. Without shoulds. Free from fear.

Warrior
Peacemaker
Philanthropist
Bridge-builder
[Your hairdresser-tool]
Explorer

This is you. This is your call. This is who you *are* and what you *do*.

Engage (commit)

A nudge. Pick one of your vocational choices above and write a job description of how *you* do this work. Give this way of life some empowering details. Imagine it. Write what you know and what you dream of … and let go of what you don't yet know. *Do one thing* today connected to this inspiring "job description."

Now, it's your turn. What or who are you beckoned to *commit to, connect with,* or *create*—whether in small or big ways?

Share something from this PoP with someone you trust.

BE BOLD. BE BRAVE. BE YOU.

Panoramic View

THERE HAVE BEEN TEN POPS CONTAINED IN LIVE ABLAZE.

Ten experiences for your unfolding story to deepen, emerge, and grow. Ten places to kindle the fire of your passions and purpose on the planet.

As we near the end of this *jOURney*, amidst the energy of this, blazing with potential and the promise of next steps and future leaps, I invite you to take a moment.

Now, my friend, reflect on your ten PoPs. If you've kept a journal, flip through its pages for more insight. Look for patterns and possibilities that have emerged out of these PoPs. Expect to be surprised. Don't force, try harder, or stress. Let go. Trust. Play.

What do you see, sense, hear? What words, ideas, or ahas? What people or places? What struggles, joys, longings, or hopes? What has emerged, popped out of the soil? What has come to life in you? What serves as kindling, lighting you up from within? What things do you want to do—differently or anew? This is the gold. Come and see.

Zoom out the lens. Imagine you're a bird flying or have a parachute strapped to your back, and gaze down at the landscape of your life from this *jOURney*, perhaps found in the pages of your journal and in your unique PoPs. Or, as if this book were a film, allow your mind to rewind and show you a picture of the different moments and scenes you've lived and experienced thus far.

Wear that explorer's hat. Look for new terrains to discover as you distill your story. In the days to come, it will continue to morph, change, and grow. But what do you see here and now, on this very day?

Whatever emerges, give it some space to breathe. What is something you can do to sit with it, to cultivate it, to explore it further? Go for a walk. Write about it. Draw or paint it. Sing or dance it. Do whatever you desire—no more, no less.

Allow the brilliance of *your* story to flourish and shine.

Keep at It

CONSIDER WHAT HAVE BEEN YOUR FAVORITE ELEMENTS OF THE POPS. DO YOU WANT TO CONTINUE TO PRACTICE YOUR POPS IN DAILY LIFE?

Is it something you plan to do at the same time(s) each day and/or on-the-fly, in response to the stressors and challenges that arise in day-to-day living?

Feel free to use the framework— *Be Still*, *Ponder*, and *Engage*—as a starting point and freely tweak it to make it your own. Consider that time to *Be Still* means not thinking, strategizing, or planning, but just *BEing*; time to *Ponder*—to reflect, to contemplate—represents going a level or two deeper into your life, panning for the gold and the glimmer within you; and time to *Engage*—to work these moments of stillness and pondering into your life—allows you to explore and experiment, doing things to see what's working and what's not, in connection with your tribe and companioned by your own relationship with the Sacred. Remember that whatever you do, never go it alone.

A daily rhythm of PoPs will nurture a life that is solid and whole, lit up with a glow that is unique to you. As your PoP practice grows, you'll find yourself using these PoPs spontaneously when life throws you a curveball—which all of us experience at one time or another. Look for ways to take the triggers that come your way during the day—worry, fear, opportunity, decisions to make, relationships to negotiate, people you love who are in pain and in need of support—and take these into a spur-of-the-moment PoP.

> A daily rhythm of PoPs will nurture a life that is solid and whole, lit up with a glow that is unique to you.

Right now, as you envision your own persistent PoPs, write about how and when you will continue this practice, including as many details as possible to direct and inspire you to solidify your PoPs and make them your own.

A nudge. Share your practice and intention with at least one person in your tribe.

(Not) The End

AS WE APPROACH THE VERY END OF THIS LEG OF OUR JOURNEY TOGETHER, THIS IS NOT THE END.

We have much left to do, together. That's good news. So keep that seatbelt fastened, dear friend. You're gonna need it.

Here and now, I invite you to partake of one last imagining that has its roots in each day of this journey. This dream is becoming more real by the moment. It is real-time. It is here and now.

You sit listening to the sea of humanity, to your sisters and brothers, near and far. You hear lilting voices, languages you do not understand. You see lands that are unfamiliar, people with whom you lock eyes. When they see you, they smile, greet you, and offer tea. Their eyes twinkle, sparkle, and beckon you to come closer, to bring others with you, to not look away. They invite you to come and sit, to rest, to feast with them.

You say yes. You let yourself go and *enJOY* the feast. *You can't not.* It's too *good.* In their company, you feel less fear and loneliness … *plentiful peace, flourishing freedom, herculean hope,* and *limitless love* are here. Right here, right now. In you and in those around you.

You hear a song … a mighty and unstoppable melody of voices is coming together. In the din, you hear it: the free, beautiful shouting of your own voice. And, among these many, you feel it: you *BElong.*

You have become a vital part of a mighty community of many others, who wade into the deep and dark places of the world, carrying the torch of hope as you go. Together, you are peacemakers, not fettered by fear of difference, the unknown, or the unfamiliar. You keep it real, speak about and listen to what really matters to one another, live *BEloved*, and fervently vow to *be love*. You are humble warriors of love and justice who *BElong* to one another.

Right here, right now, as a tribe, you celebrate one another's unique and one-of-a-kind destinies that are unstoppably growing and flourishing with jaw-dropping beauty.

Together, you live your big dreams, the ones you have dared to hope and claim as real and true. You pick up the tools that are yours to wield with innovative brilliance. You create things that make life better for those near and far. You are a tribe of makers who make a difference … you are a *kula* of changemakers.

You bask in the thrill of the thrumming of your hearts on this adventure that continues on … each and every day. This is a way of life that is yours till your last breath. This adventure has no end, and there is always more exploring to be done.

> You create things that make life better for those near and far. You are a tribe of makers who make a difference ... you are a *kula* of changemakers.

This tribe won't wait to hoot and holler its cheers until things are all figured out. Collectively, you let go and boldly celebrate and trust that your next steps will appear at just the right time and in ways that are more than you could have thought to dream of or imagine.

Together, you dare to rest, to play, to let go, to dance, to sing, to feast, to envision, to plan for, and to pour yourselves into work that you love, that sustains your lives, and that enables you to provide for those you love. You are known as those who walk the planet with unrestrained generosity, a mighty community of *EXTRAvagant* philanthropists, from the kindergarteners to the elders, from the richest to the poorest, from the haves to the have-nots. You see and claim that this is your human birthright and live it more fully every day.

Your community's gratitude is inexhaustible. It is oceanic. You have plenty and are plenty. You cherish the beauty, the hope, the *enough-ness* that is here now. You are buoyed; your loads are lightened. And about those loads—you carry these burdens together. You are burden-bearers for one another in the dark and light moments of life.

> You have become a vital part of a mighty community of many others, who wade into the deep and dark places of the world, carrying the torch of hope as you go.

You live humbly and unrestrained in your interdependence as a tribe. You bask in a steady stream of conversation with each other, as trusted soul friends. These conversations extend to include more and more of those in your human family, and with the always-with-and-for-you, Spirit.

Wow. Now, it's time to take a breath.

What's coming next is so important, dear one.

Listen. Do you hear it? The tribe of your human family has gathered and is cheering *you* on. Celebrating *you*. Cheering for *you*. Seeing *your* freedom, courage, *comPASSION*, and your fierce and unstoppable commitment to *be love*.

I am in this crowd, shouting rowdy *hurrahs* for *you*.

We wildly *whoop your* name. We rise to our feet and stomp a boisterous standing ovation for *you*. We revel in who *you* are, who *you* have become, and who *you* are yet to be. We are ecstatic and ready to keep leaping and to light up the world with *you*. The cause of our thunderous praise is crystal clear. You rock and *you are ablaze*.

So, my wondrous and extraordinary friend, buckle your seatbelt.

It's only just begun.

With a heart full-to-the-brim of great love and hope …

xo
Sarah DT

[glowing]

emitting warmth. showing radiance.
being rich and warm in color.
shining with an intense heat.

the jOURney continues

We hope this journey
has held up a mirror so that you now see yourself
and the world with new eyes,
has illuminated a long-held passion
or a brand new one,
has encouraged and inspired you,
has ignited you with a vision and strategy
for increased connection,
has energized you with a sense of
your one-of-a-kind purpose on the planet,
has filled you to the brim with curiosity,
has elevated the dignity of all,
including your own,
and
has lit you up with
hope,
love,
and joy ...
from this day forward.

You belong here.
We belong to each other.
Let's standTALL together and light up the world.

Join the Seeds Kula Collective

WELCOME, DEAR FRIEND. IF YOU'VE EVER WONDERED HOW ONE PERSON COULD POSSIBLY MAKE A DIFFERENCE JUST BY SHOWING UP EXACTLY AS THEY ARE-WELCOME TO THE SEEDS *KULA* COLLECTIVE!

We invite you to learn, expand, link arms for change, to live ablaze and light up the world. You belong here.

We are a collective of everyday people who are committed to light up the world so that a mighty difference can be made *together*. We do what we do because we believe that we belong to each other and that each and every person matters. We passionately work to make an indelible dent in global human rights *and* in one another's day-to-day lives.

We connect individuals, non-profits, government agencies, or businesses, in order to increase the ability of each to make a unique and significant impact. *Everyone* has something of value to share with others—whether time, money, voice, or purpose.

There are things for which we have each been destined that we cannot do alone. Step by step, arm in arm, we are creating a well-worn path of inspired vision and action, making mighty contributions, and offering our gifts in response to some of the world's greatest challenges.

In our community, you can rest, pause, take a breath, you can *be*. Be you.

Listen for the trumpet call to rise, to leap, to be inspired from within and by our people to say *YES!* We promise, this community will light you up. You—we—will never be the same.

You belong here.
We belong to each other.
Let's *standTALL* together
and light up the world.

Visit bit.ly/SeedsComm to sign up for stories
from around the world to inspire and ignite

seedsofexchange.org | connect@seedsofexchange.org

Facebook & Instagram @SeedsOfExchange

Read More & Journey on

SOULFULLY ABLAZE: A 40-DAY JOURNEY TO LIGHT UP YOUR LIFE (AND THE WORLD) IS A RADICALLY SIMPLE-SIMPLY RADICAL-WAY TO FUEL YOUR LIFE, STILL THE NOISE, DISCOVER YOUR NEXT STEPS, AND TO CONNECT MORE WITH OTHERS AS YOU GO.

You may choose to use it on its own or as a companion for *Live Ablaze: And Light Up the World*.

This one-of-a-kind adventure will unleash within you a new vision for your unique ways to be a vital part of the lives of those who matter most to you in your family, neighborhood, and in far-flung parts of the world. It will amplify your purpose on the planet and help you cultivate a tribe of people that will delight and surprise you. It will fan the flame of your dormant or blazing dreams. One step at a time, your life will begin to light up with an unmistakable glow. This is where the fire of your life is stoked.

The timeframe of a forty-day journey is rooted in the power of both the spiritual and scientific to notably reframe, restart, and regenerate. Each day includes a reading for soulful learning and inspiration, followed by a time of simple stillness, reflection, and nudges for unique-to-you inspired action. You will have opportunities to weave these practices with ease into more bits of your life in ways that will create plentiful peace, flourishing freedom, herculean hope, and limitless love.

soulfullyablazebook.com

grateFULL

WITHOUT Y'ALL, MY TREASURED AND TRUSTED TRIBE, THIS BOOK WOULD NOT BE ... MY TOUR GUIDE, MY LOVE IN AND FOR ALL OF LIFE, JESUS.

My extraordinary and treasured family, you are my roots: Mom & Dad, Beks Vashti Abraham E, Liz T, Aunt Deb & the Berks, Grandpa John & Grandma Marion, Grandpa & Grandma Tracy, Momma Sue & Nana, Cody & Mel & the D's, the Carlson Crew.

This book was crafted, propelled, and buoyed within a most-extraordinary collective of sistahs and brothas, my *book kula*. Donna Mazzitelli (merrydissonancepress.com), on paper, you are an editor, but, in reality, you have been part midwife, sage, teacher, shepherd, and *anam cara* (a Gaelic term for "soul friend"). You are a glittering gift. Astrid Koch (astridkoch.com), thank you for being a part of launching this story into the world with jaw-dropping beauty, clarity, and impact. 'Cuz that's just what you do. Andrea Costantine (communityforthesoul.com), you have been a champion and guide of this project since its inception, and I'm ecstatic and thankful for your part in crafting the look and feel within *Live Ablaze* to be one of experiential beauty, connection, and adventure. Polly Letofsky and Susie Schaefer (mywordpublishing.com), your fierce companioning and extraordinary expertise has made this book journey one of far greater ease, joy, and excellence than it would have been on my own. Danielle Norris (sovenco.com), not only were you the first person on the planet to read this manuscript, but your heartbeat to align strategy, impact, and humanity has been pivotal in this project and for Seeds. Amy K Wright (amykwright.com), you are tenacious in your commitment to tell stories well, and I am over-the-moon-grateful for your part in this tale. J Renae Davidson (jcreative.us), thank you for the rockin' photograph sesh—you have such a gift. Rachael Jayne and Datta Groover and Tom Bird (grooverseminars.com & tombird.com), your invitation, collaboration, and support catapulted this book into being.

My sistahs and brothas, for life: Susan & the C's, Aya & the S's, Nil H, JJ & the C's, Amy & the B's, Kathleen & the V's, Rochelle & the R's, Raquel & the PS's, Papa Jim P, Lisa & the S's, Erin & the E's, Q & the S's, Grant K, Josh D, Ryan B, Christy & the G's Raju & Samita & the S's, Hakan G, Hannah B, Ruth B, Pabitra B, Sangeeta A, Anjila SK, Jaimala G, Delta D, Astrid K, VKP, Dom DR, Helberth R, Anne E, Alexis N, Lydia D, Winter W, Aliyah J, Vaun S, Bill & Jane R, Lil', Stu S, Lima & Malika A, Marcellina & the O's, Godee & the M's, Anna & the W's, Rose & the O's, Kel & My Joe C, Fatouma & Ibrahim & the AY's, Nicole & Phil & the A's, Bill Z, Barb Y, Meg & the S's, Jorge C, Kate H. You have each played a real, true, and vital part in this story.

To the most-amazing changemakers and storytellers of *The True Cost* film team (truecostmovie.com), Shima Akhter, *Resurface* film team (resurfacethemovie.com), Operation Surf (amazingsurfadventures.biz/programs/operation-surf), Van Curaza, Bobby Lane, Vedran Smailović, Christina Noble and the Christina Noble

> Let gratitude be the pillow upon which you kneel to say your nightly prayer.
> -Maya Angelou

Children's Foundation (cncf.org), and the *band of brothers* of the #DoSomethingForNothingCampaign, Joshua Coombes, Dave Burt, and Matt Spracklen.

And, the finale of my thanks is to my beloveds. Soph and Micah, you two inspire me to my core, and the little people you are makes my heart thrum with more love than I ever imagined possible. Bran, you have been a part of each and every step of this journey, offering your clear-sighted and rock-solid vision, cheering me on unceasingly. You have been a real-life picture of fierce and extravagant love. I love you three.